Further
Computer
Appreciation

Further Computer Appreciation

T. F. Fry ACMA, AMBIM, FIDP

Head of Department of Business and Secretarial Studies
Cassio College, Watford, Herts.

BUTTERWORTHS

LONDON - BOSTON
Sydney - Wellington - Durban - Toronto

THE BUTTERWORTH GROUP

United Kingdom	Butterworth & Co (Publishers) Ltd London: 88 Kingsway, WC2B 6AB
Australia	Butterworths Pty Ltd Sydney: 586 Pacific Highway, Chatsworth, NSW 2067 Also at Melbourne, Adelaide and Perth
Canada	Butterworth & Co (Canada) Ltd Toronto: 2265 Midland Avenue, Scarborough, Ontario, M1P 4S1
New Zealand	Butterworths of New Zealand Ltd Wellington: 26−28 Waring Taylor Street, 1
South Africa	Butterworth & Co (South Africa) (Pty) Ltd Durban: 152−154 Gale Street
USA	Butterworths (Publishers) Inc Boston: 10 Tower Office Park, Woburn, Mass. 01801

First published by Newnes-Butterworths 1977
Reprinted 1978, 1979, 1980

© T. F. Fry, 1977

ISBN 0 408 00239 5

Typeset by Butterworths Litho Preparation Department

Printed in the U.S.A.

Preface

The concept of Further Computer Appreciation is, on the one hand to follow on from some of the principles discussed in Computer Appreciation and, on the other hand, to include some new aspects for which there was no room in the first book.

In the five years since Computer Appreciation was first published some examination syllabuses have been revised and expanded and it is hoped that this further text will provide students with a more comprehensive cover for these syllabuses. Examinations I have particularly borne in mind are the Royal Society of Arts Computer Appreciation, Ordinary National Certificate and Diploma in Business Studies, The Institute of Administrative Accounting and the Data Processing papers of the Institute of Cost and Management Accountants and the Association of Certified and Corporate Accountants. As with Computer Appreciation, I have tried to keep the text as simple and as non-technical as possible explaining perhaps more what is done than how it is done, and have orientated it towards the use of computers in business.

May I express my thanks to those firms who have kindly supplied illustrations and systems descriptions—I.B.M., I.C.L., K & N Electronics Ltd., Kienzle Data Systems Ltd., National Cash Registers Ltd., and Westrex Company Ltd. Finally my thanks to Marian Bentley who with admirable patience deciphered my handwriting and most efficiently typed the manuscript.

T. F. FRY

Contents

1

The Development of Computers

Little more than thirty years have passed since the commissioning of the first computer, designed and constructed at Harvard University in 1944. Over this short period of time have been developed the highly sophisticated and versatile machines in use today.

Until thirty years ago, basic principles in the design of calculating devices had changed very little during the previous 250 years. Blaise Pascal's original concept of geared cog-wheels to perform addition and subtraction was improved upon to give a multiplication and division capability by Baron Gottfried Von Leibnitz and refinements developed and added over a number of years by a succession of innovators resulted in machines technically more efficient, smaller and more convenient to use. Limited areas of automation were exploited, particularly in the areas of Punched Cards and pre-set mechanical programming devices. Machines became powered electrically rather than by hand, but the cog-wheels still turned, the levers still pushed, the pins still probed, the relays still clicked. Little fundamental change had taken place.

THE FIRST COMPUTERS

Indeed, the machine completed at Harvard University in 1944 (the Automatic Sequence Controlled Calculator (ASCC)) did not, itself, get away from these basic mechanical principles and processes. While it is generally recognised as being the first working automatic computer, it was a far cry from machines as we know them to-day. It had no electronic storage either for data or for program and the sequence in which instructions were recorded on paper tape had to be rigidly followed. It was slow, but within its limitations was a successful machine, performing the task for which it was designed for some fifteen years or so.

In 1944 John von Neuman was largely instrumental in the design and development of the first full Automatic Electronic Computer known as ENIAC—Electronic Numerical Integrator and Computer. This immense machine completed at Pennsylvania in 1946 weighing thirty tons and containing some 18000 thermonic valves had a very limited storage capacity and no facility for storing its program. Instructions had to be conveyed to the machine through the medium of wired plug boards and by setting switches. However, compared with ASCC, operating speed had decreased dramatically with a cycle time of 200 μs. Nevertheless, this machine marked the beginning of the development of truly electronic computers and, indeed, can be regarded as the first in what is often referred to as the first generation of these machines.

It was during the construction of ENIAC, in 1945, that von Neuman published his report on EDVAC (Electronic Discrete Variable Automatic Computer). This introduced the design concept of an internal electronically stored program and the idea of a machine with a storage capacity of 1000 words of 10 decimal digit capacity.

However, EDVAC was not to be built until 1950, one year after the completion of EDSAC (Electronic Delay Storage Automatic Computer) —the first Automatic Electronic Stored Program Computer—at Cambridge University. This incorporated a mercury delay line store of sixteen 35-bit words and 3800 thermionic valves. Input and output media was 5 track paper tape reading and writing at 15 c.p.s.

It was early in 1949 that Lyons, working in conjunction with Dr. Wilkes at Cambridge, decided to build a computer. Work on the machine commenced later on in the year, and incorporated a new type of storage medium, magnetic tape. The machine was known as LEO (Lyons Electronic Office) having valves and magnetic tape storage. It was completed in 1951. After trials the first application, bakeries sales evaluation, was implemented later on in the year, and in 1953 Lyons payroll was computerised on LEO I which coped with this work quite successfully until the machine was closed down in 1965.

Up until 1951, the research and development of computers was generally the exclusive province of the Universities. From this point onwards, however, office machine and electrical equipment manufacturers started to develop machines for commercial use, putting into practice the principles and techniques developed at the universities. This development included work by ICT—a combine of BTM (Hollerith) and Power Samas—to produce HEC I (Hollerith Electronic Computer) in 1951 and later, in 1953, HEC II, seven of which were marketed from 1954 onwards. The Ferranti Mark I was completed and delivered to Manchester University in 1951 and, indeed, was the first general purpose computer available commercially.

Parallel with this development in hardware, intensive work was done on *computer programming software.*

The mid-fifties saw the development of a new range of computers with new types of immediate access store—*magnetic drum* and *magnetic core* storage. At about this time a number of companies were involved in the construction and marketing of digital commercial machines, using these new developments.

The fourth version of ICT's Hollerith Electronic Computer (HEC4) was marketed as the 1201 with 1 K of store, and 1202 with 4 K of store, a total of one hundred and twenty-four of these machines being sold. English Electric produced DEUCE (Digital Electronic Universal Calculating Engine) with both magnetic drum and mercury delay line storage. IBM introduced their 700 series and Honeywell their 400 and 800 computers.

SECOND GENERATION COMPUTERS

1950 proved to be a landmark in computer technology, with the discovery of the planar silicon transistor and the incorporation of this device in the UNIVAC II machine. This point is generally recognised as the commencement of the second generation of computers. A year later in 1957, the ICT 1300 series of computers was introduced and the second edition of LEO, of which eleven machines were sold. Commercially, the most successful machine of this period was IBM's medium size machine, the 1400 series, with a virtually world wide acceptance.

As hardware developed in power, complexity and sophistication, so it became necessary to develop programming software that eliminated

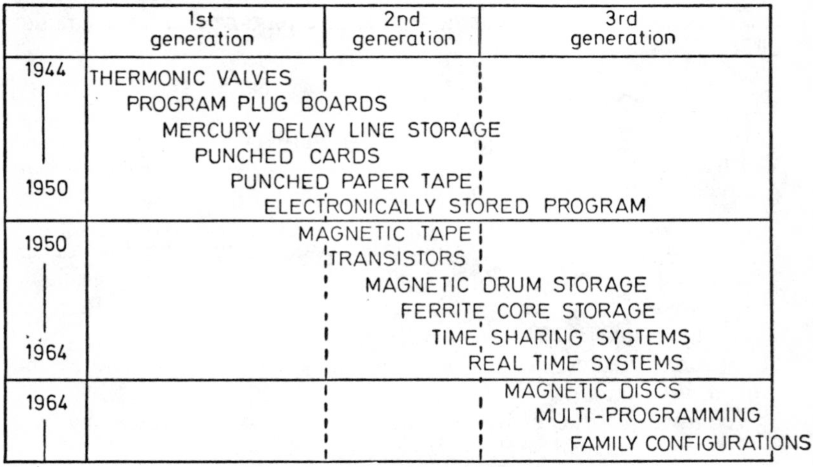

	1st generation	2nd generation	3rd generation
1944 ⋮ 1950	THERMONIC VALVES PROGRAM PLUG BOARDS MERCURY DELAY LINE STORAGE PUNCHED CARDS PUNCHED PAPER TAPE ELECTRONICALLY STORED PROGRAM		
1950 ⋮ 1964		MAGNETIC TAPE TRANSISTORS MAGNETIC DRUM STORAGE FERRITE CORE STORAGE TIME SHARING SYSTEMS REAL TIME SYSTEMS	
1964			MAGNETIC DISCS MULTI-PROGRAMMING FAMILY CONFIGURATIONS

Figure 1.1. Computer generations

the tedium and labour of program construction in machine orientated coding. Manufacturers had tended to develop their own programming codes in isolation directed to the use of their own particular machines and while a general standardisation of machine codes was impracticable due to the variance in design and construction of machines, the concept

of high level languages in which programs could be universally expressed
began to take shape. The first of these, FORTRAN, was introduced by
IBM with their 700 series machine.

The European Association for Applied Mathematics and Mechanics
and the American Association for Computing, meeting in Zurich in
1958, began research into the development of a universal programming
language and eventually produced ALGOL 60. A couple of years later
the USA government in conjunction with computer manufacturers and
users sought to develop a language specifically designed for commercial
data processing; this resulted in the introduction of the COBOL language.

New ideas were now taking shape in hardware development and use,
and we find the terms Time Sharing and Real Time being introduced.
IBM pioneered Time Sharing techniques by linking four control terminals to a 709 machine in the early sixties. This was known as Project
MAC (Multiple Access Computers).

The first machine with the capability of storing more than one
program simultaneously and to switch from program to program
according to processing demands was LEO II in 1961, from which was
later developed LEO 326 and 360 models. It was the Sabre Reservation
System for American airlines that represented the first large scale
real-time system involving some twenty-five terminals covering a radius
of 300 miles.

THIRD GENERATION COMPUTERS

In 1965/6 the third generation of computers were introduced. At
this point, problems exercising the minds of companies involved in
computer development can be summarised as:

1. To increase the versatility of configurations in the sense that advantage could be taken of any combination of the range of available
   peripherals by providing the capacity for interchange within the
   configuration.
2. To make greater use of the processing speed now provided by the
   central processor.
3. To provide *hardware* capable of meeting systems application demands
   for immediate and random access to records.
4. To develop means whereby a central computer could accept, process
   and transmit answers to a number of remote points simultaneously.
5. To provide input and output devices capable of fast and accurate
   transmission of information to and from the central processor.

Up to this stage, computer configurations tended to inflexible. For
instance a central processor of a given storage capacity with input and

output peripherals of say, a card reader and a line printer, and with magnetic tape storage, would probably remain as such with modifications to the configuration unlikely.

THE DEVELOPMENT OF PROCESSORS AND STORAGE SYSTEMS

The development and introduction of a wider range of input, output and backing storage peripherals gave rise to the need to develop central processors with interfaces capable of accepting selections from within this range at the choice of the user. This in turn meant central processor design flexible enough to enable core store capacity to be increased as required. Compatability and versatility became the keynotes in those elements making up a computer configuration, so leading to the concept of what have been called family machines. The ICT 1900 series and the IBM 360 series are examples of these.

As, in the early days of computing, input devices were no longer restricted to punched media, final output to a printed format or backing storage devices to magnetic tape. The demands of systems applications called for new input techniques, as for example magnetic ink character and optical character readers as well as direct remote on-line input. While expansion in the range of output devices was not as marked, the line printer was still generally the most suitable for commercial systems; never-the-less, for some specialised requirements visual display units or direct output to remote terminals were to play their part. In the realm of backing storage the need for large scale direct access stores had to be satisfied. This was mainly accomplished through the medium of magnetic discs.

A further development centred around the need to take the greatest advantage of the speeds at which central processors could work. For all practical purposes, processing speed is governed by the rate that information can be conveyed to the central processor on the one hand and by the rate at which information could be output on the other. The comparatively slow speed of such input and output devices meant central processing units working at only a fraction of their capacity. Multi-processing became in part an answer to this with a central processing unit capable of storing two or more programs simultaneously and switching from one to another in order to decrease the amount of time the processor was standing idle awaiting work.

While serial access backing storage devices were ideal for fast batch processing techniques, provided input records were sorted into an order compatible with those on the storage device, the time lag between the occurrence of an event and the updating of the records effected by the event was considerable. With the introduction of backing storage containing records, any one of which could be accessed in a very short time, came the concept of updating information as and when the event occurred. This necessitated the availability of an input device that could be used on the site of the occurrence. From this came the development of terminals, remote from the computer, but linked by direct line so that information transmitted could immediately be processed and, if required a response in the form of the results of processing immediately transmitted back to the terminal.

THE PRESENT POSITION

Computers in use today fall into a number of fairly well defined categories:

1. Small to medium sized configurations with core sizes around 16 K to 64 K supporting a range of peripheral devices. Backing storage of either serial or direct access type, that is magnetic tape or disc with input through punched media and output usually to a line printer. Generally used in a batch processing mode with a single stored Program. These are self-contained installations, accepting source data, performing data conversion procedures, processing files and outputting reports in hard copy form.
2. Larger configurations capable of working in a *multi-programming mode*. With a larger core store to accommodate a number of programs simultaneously and more backing storage to hold a wider range of files on-line.
3. Large *time-sharing machines* linked to users by remote terminals. These machines need high volume backing stores to hold programs that can be called in on demand and to hold a wide range of record files.
4. *Real-time systems* for up-dating records as the movement activity occurs, and for file interrogation purposes. Again these machines support remote terminals and need a large core store and high volume backing storage.
5. Machines using a *data base storage principle* where all records are held in direct access devices available on-line for use in any processing system requiring them.
6. *Dedicated machines.* These are specialised machines designed for one specific application, and it has been the development of mini and later micro solid state electronics that has widened the range of applications possible with the microcomputer minicomputer. An example is the automatic recording of point of sale transactions either through the medium of till-keyboard depressions or light pen scanning processes of coded information on product labels.

7. *Visible record computers.* These are sometimes known as *mini-computers* or *desk type computers*, and have popularity with the small and medium sized firm where requirements include a progressively updated printed record of its transactions as well as electronically recorded data for analysis purposes and for reference. The type of machine has very much gained in popularity over the past several years. A detailed account of an application on a visible record computer is given in Chapter 13.

FUTURE TRENDS

An attempt to forecast where computers go from here can only be made in the light of current developments and trends.

As far as machine sizes are concerned, the general tendency appears to be away from medium sized machines, towards very large central configurations serving a number of users remote from the machine but linked by data transmission lines. However, the other end of the spectrum should not be overlooked. The increase in the use of small visible record computers has been dramatic over the past few years and for the fairly small business are becoming increasingly popular.

Physically, central processors are tending to become smaller in size for equivalent power. This has been due to the development of mini circuitry followed by micro solid state circuitry, a process that is continuing. Research is going on into alternative kinds of immediate access store, as an alternative to ferrite cores. For example, semiconductor memory units capable of holding a thousand or more bits are becoming generally available in solid state chips.

Input and output devices of the future will tend more and more to eliminate the laborious process of converting data into a machine acceptable form. While magnetic tape character recognition and optical character recognition are already with us in limited form, the capture of data at source is the subject of a great deal of interest and research. New types of mass backing storage are the subject of research and experimentation. Will the conventional magnetic tape and magnetic disc be replaced eventually with such devices as for example mass data cartridge or electronic beam memory devices giving far larger on-line capacities, faster direct access rates, and higher data transmission speeds?

Will acoustic input and output develop from its present very limited application and become a generally used media for communicating with the machine and indeed will sensory input by attaching electrodes to our head to pick up thought waves ever become a reality?

Whatever happens, computers will continue to develop, input methods will become more direct, data banks will become more vast. Perhaps, in thirty years time computers will bear as little resemblance to the computer of today as modern computers do to the first machine at Harvard University in 1944.

EXERCISES

1. Computers are often referred to in the context of 'generations' of machines. Explain how, in substance, different generations differ from one another.

2. Give an account of the main technical developments in computer storage since the first machines were constructed using mercury delay line storage.

3. Differentiate in principle between:
   (a) Multi-programming.
   (b) Time sharing.
   (c) Real-time computer working.

4. What do you consider to be the main trends in computer development today?

5. In many computer installations, a great deal of time and work goes into the preparation of data ready for input to the computer. Suggest ways by which you feel this work could be cut down or eliminated.

2
Basic Elements and Functions

The purpose of this chapter is to introduce a few basic concepts relating to the more powerful and versatile range of digital computers that have, over the fairly recent past, been increasingly taken into use for processing data. It is not the object in this chapter to deal with the concepts in detail as this will be done in later chapters.

CATEGORIES OF DATA PROCESSING MACHINES

To attempt to classify machines into defined groups in terms of size and power, bearing in mind the very wide range of computing devices available today, is hardly practical. However, four fairly well defined categories used in business data processing can be outlined as follows.

Programmable desk calculators

These are really sophisticated electronic calculating devices with the capacity to store a very limited range and number of program instructions, and a limited range of constants. Some machines have a 'hardcopy' print-out capacity while others a digital read-out, i.e. a row of illuminated numbers in the window of the machine.

These machines are generally used as an aid in manual processing systems. They are quite fast in operation, and their use, by and large, is limited to a purely arithmetical function.

Minicomputers; visible record computers; desk top computers

These three terms are commonly used in reference to the same type of machine. This kind of computer is really a development arising from mechanical and electro-mechanical accounting machines, incorporating the advantages of electronic processing and storage. There is a wide range of machines of this type on the market, and the past two or three years has shown a rapid increase in their popularity.

Chapter 12 contains a detailed study of these computers.

TYPES OF COMPUTER

The term 'computer' can be associated with three different types of machine known as digital, analogue and hybrid computers.

In commercial data processing procedures, as we have already seen, we are concerned in manipulating data of two types, one we have called descriptive data and the other quantitative data. In both cases however, whether this information is initially expressed in alphabetic characters, symbols or digits, they have in common the fact that when they are written to store, they are all represented by a series of digits, or numbers. The numbering system we use is Binary with the need for only two digits 0 and 1. All processes are carried out in terms of these digits, whether it is just a case of moving descriptive data from one area of store to another, or carrying out some arithmetic function on quantitative data. This type of computer works in discrete numbers and is known therefore as a *digital* computer.

There are, however, two other types of computer (*analogue* and *hybrid*) which, while they are not normally used in commercial data processing, it would be helpful to include a brief description.

Analogue computers

Perhaps the easiest way to explain the difference between digital and analogue computers is by a very simple example.

If we wanted to measure, in gallons per minute, the rate of water-flow through a tap, one approach would be to place a succession of one gallon buckets under the tap, removing each as it became full, and continue to do this for 30 seconds. We could then count the number of filled buckets, multiply this by 2 and arrive at a gallons per minute flow rate. This is a digital approach to the problem. We are working in discrete numbers, 30 seconds and number of buckets full of water. This incidentally, would only give us a flow rate for one particular ½ minute in time, and ignores the fact that rate changes from one minute to another in the light of variables such as the water velocity and the tap aperture.

An alternative approach would be to fit monitoring devices that would continuously measure the water velocity and tap aperture, convert these measurements into electrical impulses, relate these in order to produce the movement of a needle over a graduated dial indicating flow rate in gallons per minute. We then have an analogue computing situation. In effect an analogue computer is concerned with the continuous measurement of physical quantities and performing computations on these measurements using, in turn, the physical properties of the computer itself to provide an analogy of the problem to be solved.

One further very simple example of this analogue function often quoted is that of a car speedometer. Here the speed indicated on the dial represents the speed of the car in miles per hour. This is arrived at, not by computing numbers, but by the continuous monitoring of shaft revolution speeds and a conversion of this through the device's physical properties, gears and cables, to give a reading on a dial.

It is not the province of this book to get involved in the technicalities of analogue computers. Sufficient to say that the applications for which they are used are mainly in the science and engineering fields and they have little relevance to commercial data processing applications.

Hybrid computers

Strictly speaking this is not another type of computer but a machine that incorporates both analogue and digital elements.

It has the advantage of providing a digital memory for storing not only constants and intermediate processing results, but also a program to direct the activities of the analogue element which would otherwise normally be programmed and operated manually. The use of both principles in problem solving requires the use of analogue-to-digital and digital-to-analogue converters, so that information can be presented in the numerical form necessary to a digital process.

Digital computers

Digital machines used in processing commercial systems can, broadly speaking, be placed in one or other of two categories:

1. Those configurations that are, by and large, designed to work in a batch processing mode. These machines would usually have a medium size core store, say 16 K to 48 K, backing storage of either sequential or direct access type, input devices to read data recorded on punch cards or punch paper tape, and have a line printer as an output device. These machines would normally be capable of running one program only at a time.
2. The larger and more powerful machines having one or more of a number of capabilities in addition to (1) above, such as multi-programming, multi-access, and a capacity to work in a real time mode as distinct to a purely batch processing mode.

In the book *Computer Appreciation* an analogy was drawn between the performance of a computer and the performance of a clerk working on a routine clerical procedure. The suggestion was made that the basic functions involved are common to both, e.g. a clerk working on pricing and extending stores requisitions would be involved with the following factors:

Receipt of requisitions from stores and the assimilation of the data contained in them   INPUT

Reference to price lists to obtain unit price of the articles	STORAGE
Calculating value—quantity X unit price	ARITHMETIC
Recording on the requisition the results of the above calculation	OUTPUT
Performing these processes in accordance with a pre-determined set of instructions	PROGRAM
Monitoring the work for accuracy etc. by the supervising clerk	CONTROL

It would be true to say that these basic functions are common to all of the types of machine listed above.

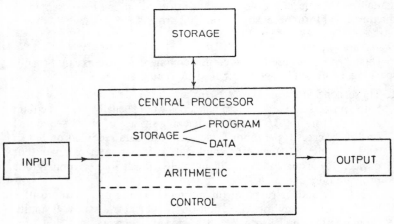

Figure 2.1. A basic computer configuration

Given then a relatively basic computer configuration as in Figure 2.1 we have the capacity to automatically process the data and obtain the same results as with the manual system, but at far greater speed.

THE CENTRAL PROCESSOR

The configuration shown in Figure 2.1 consists of a *central processor* we have the capacity to automatically process the data and obtain the the data items currently being processed, the capacity to carry out the necessary calculations and a control function. This central processor is linked with peripherals to input the data e.g. a punch card or punch paper tape reader, to output the results of processing, e.g. a line printer or a teleprinter, and with backing storage, magnetic tape or magnetic disc.

However, this is a rather simple and basic concept of a computer in that it just serves the purpose of taking over a routine manual system. Not only this, but it represents a far from efficient usage of the processing speed and power available in a central processor. Central processors work at a very high speed, their operation time is measured in millionths of a second or, in very fast modern machines, in nanoseconds, i.e. thousand-millionths of a second. On the other hand, input and output devices work at a comparatively slow speed. Given a machine with one input and one output channel, even fast magnetic tape will not provide a transfer rate fast enough to keep up with the speed at which the central processor is able to deal with the information. Indeed, for a great deal of its time, the processor will be waiting for work to get on with. If we appreciate that, in the normal commercial batch processing run, the volume of input and output data is high compared with the amount of processing involved, it will readily be seen that operating under these circumstances the processor is working at only a fraction of its full efficiency.

In using a computer solely for routine batch processing, we are faced with two limitations. Firstly, at any one time, operations are limited to this purely routine work, and the machine cannot cope with the other factors mentioned below that could well be present in a Data Processing situation. Secondly, the limited efficiency with which the central processor will work due to the relative slowness of its peripherals. A condition often referred to as 'Peripheral Bound'.

When we move into the region of the more powerful and more sophisticated computer, then we have the means to overcome these problems, at any rate, in part. The following is a brief review of some of the basic functions such a machine can provide, and these will be dealt with in greater detail in later chapters. Taken at its lowest level, a computer will use its component parts sequentially rather like this:

1. Read data and store in central processor from a *primary input device* such as a punch card or punch paper tape reader, or from backing storage, magnetic disc or tape, or a combination of both.
2. Carry out program processing requirements on this data.
3. Output the results of processing either to backing storage or in a final communicable form, say to a line printer.
4. Continue to repeat the above cycle until all data is processed.

The time scale involved in this sequential operation could well be as illustrated in Figure 2.2. From this it will be seen that for comparatively long periods of time the C.P.U. will be standing idle waiting for work.

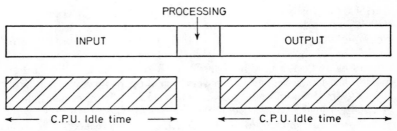

Figure 2.2. Time scale for sequential operation

One way of cutting down this idle time is by the simultaneous operation of the C.P.U. and peripheral devices, enabling processing to proceed at the same time as the input and output functions. This, in the average batch processing system, will marginally improve the efficiency of the central processor (see Figure 2.3).

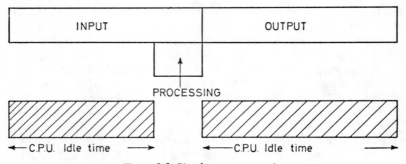

Figure 2.3. Simultaneous operation

Nevertheless, even using this principle of simultaneous operation, the central processor is still idle for a substantial proportion of the time.

MULTI-PROGRAMMING

In order to overcome these basic problems, modern medium and large size computers generally have the capacity to run two or more programs virtually simultaneously. This technique is known as *dual programming* or *multi-programming.* In principle, it involves storing two or more programs concurrently in the C.P.U. Immediate Access Store, or, in some circumstances, in Random Access Backing Storage for rapid transfer to the C.P.U. on demand.

Having then executed a series of processing instructions contained in one program, (a), instead of waiting for additional data before commencing another processing cycle, control is switched through the operating system to the second program, (b), and processing instructions from this executed. In turn, if no data is available for either (a) or (b) a third program (c) is called in, and so on. Thus, far more effective use is made of C.P.U. processing time.

Of course, such a system involves some decision making capacity to determine which program should be called in as and when processing time becomes available. This is done through a priority system written into the machine control program, so that available time is allocated to the program with the highest priority that is able to get on with its work.

One major disadvantage in batch processing is the time lag between the occurrence of an event and the recording of its effect on a given situation. For instance, the collection of movement data, invoices, credit notes, payments etc. for a purchase ledger system over a period of one week, and then their application to a master purchase ledger file in an up-dating run, means that the information on the file is never really up-to-date. Indeed, just before an up-dating run, the file would only indicate the position as it was one week previously. If we have a machine into which we can feed data as and when it occurs, and then up-date master data on file immediately, these files will reflect the true position at any time. The term given to this form of operation is *Real Time Processing.*

Real Time Processing

A *Real Time System,* in effect, is a system that accepts data relating to an occurrence at the time it takes place, processes it, and reports on the effect of the occurrence quickly enough for it to be modified. Obviously, the response time, i.e. the time between the data originating and the feedback of the results of the occurrence giving rise to the data, will vary with the purpose of the system. For example, to effect the flight of a missile, data relating to its performance would have to be processed and fed back in a matter of micro-seconds, while the effect of a cheque presented at a bank on the customer's account balance could well justify a delay in feed-back of a minute or two.

The hardware and software used in this type of system will, therefore, depend on the requirements of the system in terms of the acceptable delay in receiving processed information back. It will be appreciated that one essential condition to the operation of a Real Time System is that there should be a direct link between the point of origin of the data to be processed and the computer, and that the results of processing should be transmitted immediately and directly to the point at which the information is required. Such a method of transmitting data to and from a computer is known as 'on-line' working. The type of device used to initially transmit data and finally to receive the results of processing will, of course, vary from system to system. The technique and devices involved are more fully discusses in Chapter 4 'Input Media and Devices'.

Multi-access

Accepting then the concept of a computer directly linked to record, assess, and report on changes in a given environment, we can perhaps extend our thinking to a machine linked to a multiple number of points. Each of these points would be capable of transmitting and receiving information independently, and, if necessary, for all practical purposes, simultaneously. Such a computer system has what is known as a *multi-access* capability.

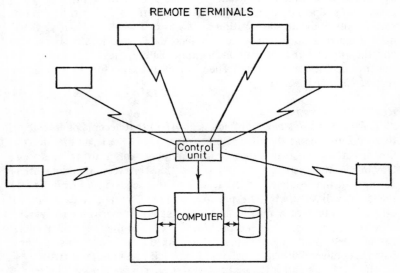

Figure 2.4. Multi-access capability

The machine is linked 'on-line', either by direct transmission line or through the Post Office telephone network, to a number of out-stations or terminals, each able to operate independently transferring data to the computer, and able to work in Real Time, so as to evoke very rapid response from the machine (see Figure 2.4). A practical example of this is where the terminal could be used to interrogate files held centrally, as in a banking system to ask for the balance on a given customer's account. Again, in multi-access techniques, the type of terminal will, of course, depend on the requirements of the system.

Generally speaking, multi-access is taken to mean a situation in which all terminal users are accessing the same files for up-dating and interrogation purposes. However, the situation often occurs, particularly with computer bureaus having a powerful machine and terminals sited in customer premises, that each user will have their own files to refer to, and will probably be using a number of different computer languages.

Under these circumstances, the computer installation is said to be working on a *time sharing* basis. This means that computer time is allocated in very short periods to the users. The program demanded for any specific process is read out of backing storage into the central processor. In some systems, files may have to be manually mounted on tape or disc transporters, but in a modern system it could well be that all files are kept on line on direct access storage devices, so as to be immediately available for use.

Multi-processing

One further term should be introduced in this survey of the facilities offered in large scale computing; this is *multi-processing*. This usually refers to a situation where a number of computers are connected to each other. The most common example is when a large computer is connected with smaller 'Slave Computers'. While the 'Slave' machine would probably be able to act in a 'stand-alone' capacity for very simple processing jobs, it would depend upon the power of the large central machine for most of its processing requirements. Indeed, it would be usual to have all data files and programs stored in the large central configuration, so that the slave worked in a real time multi-programming relationship with the master machine.

A typical slave computer might consist of a small central processor with, say, 4 K of store, a card or paper tape reader, a line printer, and a tele-printer. Thus its processing in a 'stand-alone' capacity would be extremely limited by the small size of its core store, but it would have the facility for very rapid transfer of data to and from the central machine.

PROCESSING COMMERCIAL DATA

In a computer system concerned with large scale processing of commercial data, four defined stages can be identified, see Figure 2.5. These are:

1. Capture the data at source, that is, recording in some way or another the data relating to a given occurrence as and when it happens.

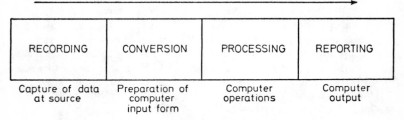

Figure 2.5. Stages of processing data

2. Preparation of the data in a form that is acceptable to the computer, and that can be read into the computer store through, for instance, a card reader or a punched paper tape reader.
3. Performance of the processing requirements on the data as determined by the program.
4. The communication of the results of processing in an acceptable form.

However, having said this, we must make one reservation. Under some circumstances, stages (1) and (2) may coincide, as for example, in the capture of data on an O.C.R. document that can be read into the computer store without need for further data preparation.

This leads us to consider the mechanics of the transference of data from the point at which it is captured to the point at which it is stored, either in the C.P.U. or in backing storage ready for processing. By nature, the type of commercial activity we require to record occurs at points distant from the computer installation, and there is, therefore, a need to transfer the data arising from such activity, from its point of origin to the computer. For example:

Data relating to the movement of stock could well originate in a store.
Data relating to sales, in an invoice department.

Data relating to the receipt of cash, in a cashier's office.
This gives rise to a need to bring all this data together to a central point—the computer room—so that processing can take place.

Now in order to minimise the need to transfer data over long distances, the sensible thing to do would be to site the computer as near as possible to those points at which the events take place that give rise to the data. However to do this, it pre-supposes that all data originates in a fairly concentrated area which in many large commercial undertakings, is not so. Branches, depots, offices, factories, and distribution points could well be scattered over a very wide area and, perhaps, throughout the country.

This gives us two alternatives. Either to site a number of small computers at these scattered points to process the data arising locally, in which case data need be transferred over only very limited distances, or to instal a central computer system to cope with the total processing needs of the organisation as a whole. In this latter case, we would obviously be involved in the transfer of data over quite long distances.

Now, while this second alternative has an inherent disadvantage arising from the need to transfer data over these long distances, obvious advantages in this approach centre around economy in hardware and a centralised source of information relating to the organisation as a whole. This leads to far greater efficiency in the control of the activities of the organisation.

The term generally used for this process of transferring data from one point to another, usually from a remote originating location to a computer installation, is *data transmission.*

DATA TRANSMISSION

This term, in its widest sense, refers to the transmission of data from a remote source, and is generally taken to mean data that is transmitted in a machine acceptable form. There are basically three ways of going about this:

(a) When data is physically transferred from source to a computer installation.
(b) When communication lines are used to transmit data to an off-line machine at the computer installation.
(c) When data is transmitted over communication lines direct to the computer.

Many instances of the physical transfer of data will spring to mind such as the G.P.O. postal service or courier and messenger services, all of which involve an appreciable amount of time in carrying the recording medium from one point to another. A common example is in the production of punched paper tape as a by-product of, say, the preparation of invoices on an accounting machine at remote branches of an organisation. The tape then being forwarded by post or messenger to a central computer for processing.

When we think of the virtually instantaneous transfer of data between two points in the form of electrical pulses, we usually refer to it as Automatic Data Transmission. We have already seen, when discussing input services, that when data is recorded in the form of punched cards or punched paper tape, on passing through a reader for storage in the central processor, the coded holes are converted into a series of electrical pulses representing 'bits'. Automatic data transmission is basically an extension of this principle applied to greater distances, with the exception that in some cases the transmitted bits may be converted back into, say, punched paper tape form and then read into the central processor. In other cases, the 'bits' may be read direct into the central processor without this reconversion process. In the first case we can say that data is being transmitted *off-line,* and in the latter case, *on-line.*

Having said that data transmission by means of communication lines is virtually instantaneous, it will be appreciated that the time taken to transmit a given volume of data will depend on the degree of operating efficiency of the conducting medium over which transmission takes place. The unit used to define the rate of transmission is known as a *'baud'.* A baud represents the transference of one bit per second.

Automatic data transmission usually makes use of the G.P.O. public telegraph or telephone networks although, in some cases, private direct lines are used. Indeed such transmissions can take place by the use of radio links including communication satellites.

The use of telegraph lines, known as the Post Office DATEL 100 service, is not generally regarded as a suitable transmission medium for computer data. As the title indicates, the speed of transmission is slow, limited to 100 bauds, and generally speaking, the conducting medium is of low quality. The Post Office telephone network offers a faster and more reliable medium at varying speeds. These are known as DATEL 200, 300, 600 and 2400 services. These numbers indicate the maximum transmission speed in bauds.

Any manufacturer's code can be transmitted on these higher speed telephone network Datel services by using suitable transmission and receiving terminals, designed to deal with the particular code used. These terminals are linked to the telephone network by means of a Post Office device known as a *modem.* This accepts the pulses from the transmitting terminal, modulates them into signals suitable for transmission over telephone lines, and then in turn demodulates back again for input to the receiving terminal.

One other device that may be used in automatic data transmission as an alternative to Modems, is an Acoustic Coupler to link terminals with the Post Office network. Instead of modulating the pulses coming from a terminal, the coupler converts them into audio signals, so that when the instrument is coupled to an ordinary telephone handset, the signals are transmitted in much the same way as ordinary voice transmission. One important disadvantage in the use of this technique is the slow maximum transmission rate of about 110 bauds.

EXERCISES

1. Explain how an analogue computer differs from a digital computer. Give an example of an application of the use of an analogue machine.

2. What are the main elements of a central processing unit? Explain briefly how each plays its part in processing data.

3. What do you understand by computer peripherals? Suggest three types of peripheral and give a short explanation of their use.

4. The term 'peripheral bound' is often used in connection with computer processing. What do you understand by this term? Explain ways in which this condition can be alleviated.

5. What is meant by data transmission? Give a short account of three different ways by which data can be transmitted to a computer.

6. Differentiate between 'on-line' and 'off-line' giving examples of on-line and off-line devices.

3

Computer Arithmetic

In recording information we are involved in the use of three sets of symbols. Digits within the range 0–9 for recording numbers, letters A–Z, and a range of symbols, for example Π + etc. In the central processor store, all of these symbols are expressed in a common coding system using two characters only, which for convenience we can express as 0 and 1. It is the combination of these two characters that identify the digit, letter or symbol represented, and is known as the binary system.

NUMBER SYSTEMS

While basically all information in a computer is held in terms of 0 and 1, there are a number of ways in which these characters can be grouped, using as a base different number systems. The following is a brief account of the more commonly used techniques.

Pure binary

As we have seen, a binary number system is one that essentially is based on a power, or Radix, of 2 and therefore only two characters are needed in its representation.

Place values in a Decimal expression are
...... $10^4, 10^3, 10^2, 10^1, 10^0$
While in a Binary expression they are
...... $2^4, 2^3, 2^2, 2^1, 2^0$
This means that the decimal expression 11111 is evaluated as:
$(1 \times 10^4) + (1 \times 10^3) + (1 \times 10^2) + (1 \times 10^1) + (1 \times 10^0)$
= 10,000 + 1,000 + 100 + 10 + 1 = 11111
While the binary expression 11111 is evaluated as
$(1 \times 2^4) + (1 \times 2^3) + (1 \times 2^2) + (1 \times 2^1) + (1 \times 2^0)$
= 16 + 8 + 4 + 2 + 1 = Decimal 31

Conversion of decimal numbers to binary can be done by successive divisions by 2, a remainder of 1 becoming a binary 1, and a zero remainder becoming a binary 0.

Example: To convert Decimal 343 to Binary.

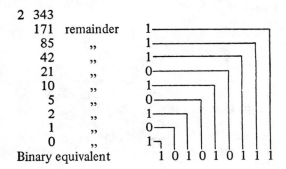

```
2  343
      171   remainder   1
       85       ,,       1
       42       ,,       1
       21       ,,       0
       10       ,,       1
        5       ,,       0
        2       ,,       1
        1       ,,       0
        0       ,,       1
```

Binary equivalent   1 0 1 0 1 0 1 1 1

To convert binary to decimal the value is equal to the sum of the value of the binary digits.

Example: To convert binary number 111011 to decimal.

$$
\begin{aligned}
& 1 \quad 1 \quad 1 \quad 0 \quad 1 \quad 1 \\
=\ & 2^5 + 2^4 + 2^3 + 0 + 2^1 + 2^0 \\
=\ & 32 + 16 + 8 + 0 + 2 + 1 = \text{decimal } 59
\end{aligned}
$$

In the above, all of the numbers used are whole numbers, or integers, but the same principle applies with fractional numbers.

Place values in a decimal fraction are

$$10^{-1}, 10^{-2}, 10^{-3}, 10^{-4} \dots\dots$$

While in a binary expression they are

$$2^{-1}, 2^{-2}, 2^{-3}, 2^{-4} \dots\dots$$

The decimal fraction .1111 is evaluated as

$$
\begin{aligned}
& (1 \times 10^{-1}) + (1 \times 10^{-2}) + (1 \times 10^{-3}) + (1 \times 10^{-4}) \\
=\ & \frac{1}{10} + \frac{1}{10 \times 10} + \frac{1}{10 \times 10 \times 10} + \frac{1}{10 \times 10 \times 10 \times 10} \\
=\ & .1 + .01 + .001 + .0001 = .1111
\end{aligned}
$$

The binary fraction .1111 is evaluated as

$$(1 \times 2^{-1}) + (1 \times 2^{-2}) + (1 \times 2^{-3}) + (1 \times 2^{-4})$$
$$= \frac{1}{2} + \frac{1}{2 \times 2} + \frac{1}{2 \times 2 \times 2} + \frac{1}{2 \times 2 \times 2 \times 2}$$
$$= \frac{1}{2} + \frac{1}{4} + \frac{1}{8} + \frac{1}{16}$$
$$= .5 + .25 + .125 + .0625 = \text{decimal } .9375$$

Any number then, however large the integer or degree of accuracy required in the fraction, can be expressed in one series of binary characters, known as pure binary.

Negative binary expressions are usually held in store in complementary form so as to enable the computer to carry out subtraction and division by complementary addition. The complement of a binary expression is found by reversing the bits and adding 1.

Find the complement of	1 0 1 1 0 1
reverse bits	0 1 0 0 1 0
add	1
True complement =	0 1 0 0 1 1

In storing information in the computer we are faced with a number of constraints which have an important bearing on the number of digits we can conveniently use for representing information. One of these is the high cost of core store with the resultant need for economy in its use. Another is the word size which in many machines is of a fixed length and can therefore only contain a specified number of binary bits. However, these considerations may be incompatible with the need to store, on the one hand very large numbers, and on the other hand to express decimal fractions to a very high degree of accuracy. The following systems, tend, in varying degrees, to overcome these problems.

Binary coded decimal

One disadvantage in the use of pure binary expression is that is can be wasteful of storage space. If, for instance, we are using a machine with a fixed word length of 24 bits, this will hold a positive binary number with a maximum value of 2^{24-1} or a negative number of 2^{23-1}.

These are numbers of such large magnitude that their use would rarely be required. Bearing in mind that the number 100 000 would only occupy 17 bits, this would leave 7 redundant bits recording insignificant O's in the word. Because most of the numbers used in commercial data processing systems are relatively small in magnitude, one can see that the use of a complete word to store each individual number would indeed be very wasteful (Figure 3.1).

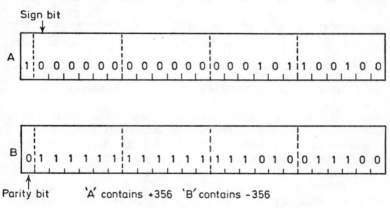

Figure 3.1. 24 Bit word recording +356
24 Bit word recording −356

An alternative way of recording numbers in store using the basic binary principle, is to convert each individual decimal digit into its binary equivalent rather than converting the whole number into a continuous binary string. The decimal number 359 for example, in pure binary would be 101100111. Converting each individual digit to binary gives:

$$
\begin{array}{ccc}
3 & 5 & 9 \\
11 & 101 & 1001
\end{array}
$$

If, then, we wish to store the number 359 in a computer store with a fixed word length of 24 bits we can either use the whole word to contain the expression 101100111—this would lead to space wasted in recording a large number of insignificant zeros—or, if the word is divided into groups of 6 bits use three groups to hold 0011, 0101 and 1001 leaving one group of six bits that could possibly be used for storing something else (Figure 3.2).

This argument, however, is only valid up to a certain point. To take an extreme example the number 2, 147, 483, 647 could be contained in a 32 bit word in pure binary while, expressed in binary coded decimal a total, including signs, of 10 groups of 4 bits would be necessary, i.e. a total of 40 bits. We can therefore conclude that for large numbers the

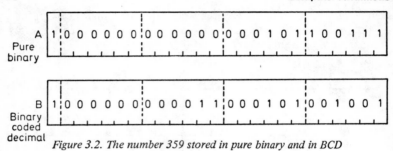

Figure 3.2. The number 359 stored in pure binary and in BCD

use of pure binary expressions could well be economical, but for smaller numbers less storage space is required for expressions in BCD form.

Another feature in using groups of bits in this way is with a group size of six, it becomes capable of representing not only the range of decimal digits (0–9) but also alphabetic characters and symbols, by giving, within a group of six bits a range of 63 different bit patterns so that this number of characters can each be given their own unique code.

Octal number system

As the name suggests this is a number system with a radix of 8 needing therefore 8 symbols only, 0–7, to represent any number. The digit position values in an octal system are

. . . . $8^3, 8^2, 8^1, 8^0$ radix point $8^{-1}, 8^{-2}, 8^{-3}$ . . . .

with the decimal equivalent of

. . . . .512, 64, 8, 1 radix point $\dfrac{1}{8}$ $\dfrac{1}{64}$ $\dfrac{1}{512}$ . . . .

Conversion of decimal to octal

The same principle is used as in the conversion of decimal to binary. Successive divisions by 8, rather than 2 as in binary, with the remainder from each division building the octal expression from right to left.

Example: To convert 6199 decimal to octal

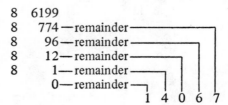

and of course, in reverse, the decimal equivalent of octal 14067 is

$$
\begin{array}{rl}
7 \times 8^0 = 7 \times 1 & = \quad 7 \\
+ \ 6 \times 8^1 = 6 \times 8 & \quad 48 \\
+ \ 0 \times 8^2 = 0 \times 64 & \quad \ 0 \\
+ \ 4 \times 8^3 = 4 \times 512 & \quad 2048 \\
+ \ 1 \times 8^4 = 1 \times 4096 & \quad 4096 \\
\hline
& \quad 6199
\end{array}
$$

Why the use of octal numbering system in computers? When discussing binary coded decimal earlier it was decided that any digit of the 10(0–9) needed to express a decimal number, could be recorded by any 4 bits with the pattern 0000 (decimal 0) to 1001 (decimal 9). Within a range of 4 bits, however, we can get 16 different patterns 0000–1111 which means the use of BCD is uneconomic in that 6 of these patterns are not being used. Now if we reduce the grouping to three bits, this gives us a range of 8 patterns 000–111 in which we can record the decimal equivalent of 0–7, in other words, an octal system. Thus a more efficient and economic use of core space is rendered possible by the use of this numbering system. When use is made of octal in this form, i.e. to record in groups of three bits the binary equivalent of a decimal digit within the range 0–7, this system is known as *binary coded octal*.

We can indeed go a stage further than this and argue, why not use the 4 bit grouping necessary for BCD working, but use a numbering system based on a radix of 16 so that all combinations of bits within the group are used. This is known as a hexadecimal system. One problem of course is that, using a system with a radix of 16, the number of symbols needed to express it is 16 and the maximum number we have in our decimal system is 10, 0–9. Of course, additional symbols can be used to represent the other 6 numbers, for example, A = 10, B = 11, C = 12 and so on.

Comparing the capacity of a 24 bit word in terms of either binary coded decimal or binary coded octal, we have then this position. The word divided into six 4 bit groupings would record in BCD as follows:

1001	1001	1001	1001	1001	1001
9	9	9	9	9	9

Giving a maximum capacity of 999 999.
While divided into eight 3 bit groupings,

111	111	111	111	111	111	111	111
7	7	7	7	7	7	7	7

giving a maximum capacity of 6 725 600.

While again 6 four bit groupings in a 24 bit word would record in Hexadecimal.

1111	1111	1111	1111	1111	1111
15	15	15	15	15	15

Decimal equivalent 122 042 240.

Floating point decimal
   If we take as an example a decimal number, say 346.258, we see this has three elements. In the centre of the expression is a decimal point to the left of which the figures express whole numbers known as an integer, and to the right a fraction. The size of the integer can be increased by the addition of figures to the left and there is no limit to the number of digits that can be so used, while the accuracy of the fraction can be increased by the addition of numbers to the right, again up to infinity.
   However, while there is no limit to the number of digits that can be used in a numeric expression, there is a limit to the medium on which it can be recorded. For instance, there is a limit to the number of characters that can be printed on this page. If therefore, we are working in large numbers with a limited size storage medium in which to hold them, a method of expressing the number in a shorter form would be both economic and convenient.
   To go back to our number quoted above, i.e. 346.258. To evaluate this, we need to know the value of each of the digits contained in the expression. In this case, since this is a decimal number each digit can be evaluated in terms of powers of 10, thus reading from left to right, the values are

$$3 \times 10^2 = 300$$
$$4 \times 10^1 = 40$$
$$6 \times 10^0 = 6$$
$$2 \times 10^{-1} = .2$$
$$5 \times 10^{-2} = .05$$
$$3 \times 10^{-3} = .008$$
$$\overline{\,346.258}$$

This base of 10 to which we are working in a decimal system is known as the radix. Since the term *decimal point* applying in this case to the point dividing the integer from the fraction, is only a true description in a decimal system, the term used to describe the point dividing the integer from the fraction in any number system is the radix point. In any number system, then, the value can be expressed as

$$\ldots\ldots R^4, R^3, R^2, R^1, R^0 \text{ radix point } R^{-1}, R^{-2}, R^{-3}, R^{-4} \ldots\ldots$$

where R equals the radix.

The small figures are known as the exponent, that is the number of times the radix must be multiplied by itself to produce the unit value of the digit in that position.

The number we are looking at, 346.258, is known as a fixed point number in that we have grouped one set of symbols around a radix point. Had the number been an integer (whole number) only, then

DECIMAL FIXED-POINT NUMBER	DECIMAL FLOATING-POINT NUMBER	DECIMAL FLOATING-POINT NUMBER WITH RADIX (10) ASSUMED
4.5678	45678×10^{-4}	45678, -4
45.678	45678×10^{-3}	45678, -3
4567.8	45678×10^{-1}	45678, -1
45678000000	45678×10^{6}	45678, 6
BINARY FIXED-POINT NUMBER	BINARY FLOATING-POINT NUMBER	BINARY FLOATING-POINT NUMBER WITH RADIX (2) ASSUMED
1.1111	11111×2^{-4}	11111, -4
11.111	11111×2^{-3}	11111, -3
1111.1	11111×2^{-1}	11111, -1
11111000000	11111×2^{6}	11111, 6

Figure 3.3. Floating point representation

the radix point would have been assumed i.e. 346. If it is a fraction only, or a mixed number, with both an integer and fractional part, then the radix point must be explicit, i.e. 0.258 or 346.258.

However, there is another way of expressing numbers using an additional set of symbols, for example $346_{10}{}^6$ or $0.258_{10}{}^4$. These are known as floating point numbers. They each have in common (a) a fixed point number, in the former being an integer the point is assumed (b) a radix number which in this case since they are both decimal expressions is 10, and an exponent.

Significant digits is the name by which the fixed point number can be known, although it is sometimes referred to as the argument or mantissa.

The evaluation of a floating point number into a fixed point representation is arrived at by multiplying the significant digits by the radix to the power of the exponent. Examples of these expressions and their conversion is given in Figure 3.3. It will be noted in these examples that the radix is assumed for binary representation. There is no need to define this as all numbers in store are held in binary.

From this it will be evident that an integer, fraction or a mixed number can be expressed in far fewer digits than its expression in significant digits, giving a marked saving of core storage space.

EXERCISES

1. Explain the difference between a number expressed in pure binary and in binary coded decimal. Show how, in both ways, the number 426 would appear in a 24-bit word containing four 6-bit bytes.

2. What do you understand by floating point decimal representation? What advantage is there in holding numbers in this form in a computer?

3. Describe how a computer accomplishes the four basic arithmetic functions, add, subtract, multiply and divide.

4. Express the following decimal numbers in pure binary.
    (a)   12.5
    (b)   19.25
    (c)   41.75
    (d)   64.375

5. Convert the following binary numbers to decimal expressions:
    (a)   11.1
    (b)   101.01
    (c)   1011.101
    (d)   1101.111

6. What do you understand by an octal number system? Show how the octal expression 13276 could be expressed using binary digits.

4

Input Media and Devices

In an area of work involving the processing of data, three essential factors must be present:

An Input—A Processing Function—An Output

This basic principle applies whether the medium for processing is a purely mental activity, manual recording, involves the use of mechanical or electro-mechanical devices or through a computer.

One basic condition that must be satisfied in every case if the processing cycle is to be successful, is that the form of the input must be compatible with the ability of the processing function to understand and to act upon it. This constraint naturally imposes limitations on the range of media that can be used for communicating information. Input to a manual typewriter, for instance, is limited to the depression of its keys, and input to a punched card tabulator is confined to the specific punched cards which the tabulator has been designed to operate.

With a computer, however, while these constraints and limits are still evident, we have a machine that can be designed to accept input information from a fairly wide range of different media. Bearing in mind that the basic mode of storage in a computer is in binary form, if one can provide the mechanics to take information in the form in which it is recorded at source and convert it into a series of binary pulses, we then have the means to convey to the machine the information upon which it is required to work.

Thinking in terms of commercial data processing by computers, there are a number of ways by which data can be fed into the central processing unit which may be sub-divided broadly into the following categories:

1. Document Reading.
2. Keyboard Devices.
3. Magnetic Media.
4. Buffer Stores.
5. Optical and Acoustic Input.

From an overall point of view, however, we must bear in mind that a multiple number of stages may well be involved between the point at which data originates to the point at which it is converted and assembled into a form acceptable for processing. When data is first created, in whatever form, it is usually referred to as source data, and the techniques of this conversion process into a machine acceptable form will

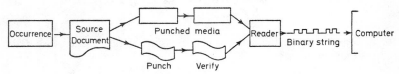

Figure 4.1. Source to machine conversion

depend mainly on two factors: (a) the form in which it originates and (b) the hardware available in the particular configuration in which the data is to be processed. For example, data recorded on a hand-written source document could well have to pass through the stages illustrated in Figure 4.1 before processing can commence.

DOCUMENT READING
    Again we can divide this form of computer input into two main categories of document.
    (a) Those that represent an intermediate stage between the source document and the computer:
        Punched cards
        Punched paper tape
        Magnetic stripe cards
    (b) Those on which source data can be directly encoded and so represent a single stage input:
        Magnetic ink character recognition
        Optical character recognition
although, as we shall see in practice it is possible to use some of these input documents in either mode.

Punched cards and punched paper tape
    Until the advent of punched cards and punched paper tape, input into devices for recording and manipulating data was by manual means. For example, the depression of keys on an accounting machine or the setting of levers on a calculating device. Punched media brought a new concept to the field of data processing by providing a means of recording data that was machine readable. The early computers used punched tape or punched cards as input media and even though machines have grown

far more sophisticated and powerful, these are still the most widely used input form.

The two methods have in common the fact that data is encoded in the form of punched holes. These holes are read by machines that sense the pattern of holes representing each character and convert these into the relevant string of binary pulses for storage in the computer.

In large scale data processing the use of punched paper tape does not represent a very flexible method of recording data. This is because records punched on a continuous strip of paper are incapable of being sorted into a defined order before being read, and it is difficult to make additions, deletions and corrections. Punched cards have, therefore, become the generally used method of recording data in punched mode.

Cards are used in a number of different ways. These are illustrated in Figure 4.2. The illustration shown in (a) is a card containing a range of characters recorded in the conventional way and (b) shows a card containing a multiple number of records punched from source documents. Figure 4.2(c) is a card used in a different mode as a source document. Information is marked in the relevant portions, and then automatically punched by a machine that will sense the position of the marks.

Cards of varying capacities have been used to record data, but the tendency has been to standardise, for computer work, on an 80-column card, i.e. a card that will record 80 characters. However, in recent years, new developments have appeared on the market, both for general data recording in punched form and for specialised applications.

Micro punched cards

Punched cards of the 80 column type generally in use are really a legacy from the old punched card data processing systems used quite extensively before the advent of computers. In as much as the development of computers for commercial processing was, to a large extent, in the hands of the manufacturers of punched card equipment, it was natural, for economic as well as practical reasons, that the existing range of punched card preparation hardware be used for computer input. Whether, given a completely free field, cards would have developed in this format is debatable. The present 80 column card is a fairly bulky and comparatively expensive medium on which to record up to 80 characters.

Recently cards very much smaller and with the same recording capacity have been coming on to the market. While the basic principle of recording data in 'hole-code' form has not changed, it brings the promise of a range of much smaller punched card equipment that could well be more convenient and cheaper to buy and to operate.

34

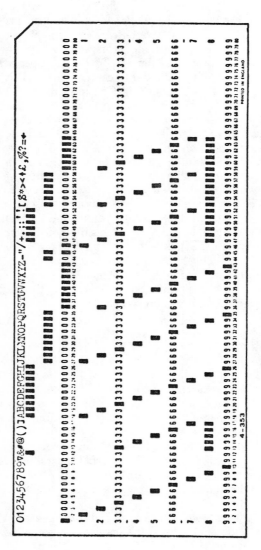

Figure 4.2(a). 80-column punched card

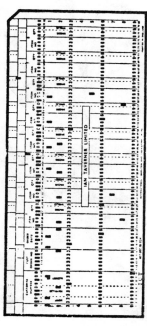

Figure 4.2(b). A spread (multi-record) punched card

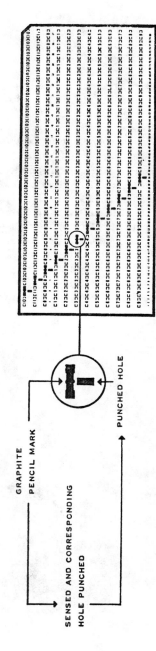

GRAPHITE
PENCIL MARK

SENSED AND CORRESPONDING
HOLE PUNCHED

PUNCHED HOLE

Figure 4.2(c). Punched card, showing mark for punched hole

Point of sales data recording

This is another area of computer input that has been the subject of research over the past few years. One major problem in direct recording of sales, particularly in retail outlets, is dealing with the vast number and range of articles that are held in stock. Three different approaches are worth mentioning briefly.

(a) *The use of small prepunched tickets that can be fixed to items and detached when they are sold.* The applications are fairly limited and used mainly to record the sale of garments. The tag contains data in punched form identifying the item, sometimes recording the price, and any other control information that may be required for sales analysis purposes. Cards are read through small purpose-built card readers and the data transferred to tape ready for computer input. Since large numbers of identical articles are likely to be held in stock, cards containing identical data can be punched automatically in quantities obviating the need for detailed and lengthy verification procedures.

(b) *Recording sales data through cash-tills.* This again is a development of traditional ways of recording sales, indeed facilities have always

Figure 4.3. Point of sales recording (National Cash Registers Ltd.)

existed for a degree of analysis by the manipulation of keys on the face of the till, summaries being printed out on tally-rolls at the end of the day. Recording sales data in a machine readable form for computer processing is now possible by writing direct, through the keyboard, to magnetic tape cassettes. The two main problems, however, are the degree of analysis available and the question of accuracy. By the nature of the system, the greater the degree of analysis called for the more the number of key entries required, or the greater the number of actual keys there must be on the keyboard. To identify, for example, each sale item down to a fine level of product code, a fairly lengthy group of characters need to be keyed in representing the code.

Two major limiting factors arise, firstly the virtual impossibility of verifying data keyed in and secondly, bearing in mind the pressures evident at busy times in a retail store, the greater the number of key depressions for each item sold, the greater the chance of inaccuracies. The delay caused by involved key entries is a further factor that is usually unacceptable.

This type of point-of-sales recording is, therefore, usually restricted to analysis on a very broad base, a small number of major product groups, each group selected by an individual till key.

(c) *Automatic point of sales recording.* If systems could be devised in which prices and control information are recorded on each product item in a way that could be automatically read when passed through a 'paying station' the need for manual recording would no longer exist. Such systems, for retail sales, have been introduced in a small number of large stores, although its widespread use has yet to be adopted.

Methods vary, but basically it consists of a printed code, usually a group of lines, or bars, of various thickness and spacing to represent binary coding. These can then be scrutinised optically or magnetically with a device that generates a pattern of pulses causing the data to be recorded on a computer input medium. Validation procedures within the reading device will signal any mis-reading so that a second attempt can be made.

There are obvious problems of scale in a large retail outlet. These are mainly due to the task of getting codes on each individual item, although encoding at the label printing stage is a solution when volumes justify this, and also the positioning of the encoding to facilitate rapid reading. Reading is usually accomplished by the use of a portable hand device that is moved over the coding.

Magnetic stripe cards

It is arguable whether this form of data input represents a medium for recording source data in a machine orientated form or a conversion stage between that and the recording of data at source. It really falls into both categories.

This form of input consists of a card on the front of which data is directly and visibly recorded through the medium of a keyboard machine. Incorporated on the card is a magnetic stripe on which the same data is encoded together with any recurring control information. This type of input has a quite specialised application in the use of small Visible Record Computers. These are dealt with in a later chapter where a more detailed explanation is given.

MICR and OCR documents

These, in contrast to punched card and punched paper tape represent input media that usually combine the source data recording function and the machine input function. They are documents on which formalised characters are printed which, when passed through a magnetic field in the case of the former and a light source in the latter case, generate waveforms. These can be identified on comparison with standard waveforms built into the circuitry of the reader and thus, on identification be converted into the appropriate binary pattern for storage in the computer.

Examples of MICR and OCR founts are shown in Figure 4.4 and also an illustration of an OCR document used in a mark sensing mode.

Bearing in mind that the final input mode into the computer is in binary form, that data usually originates in digital form, and that a great deal of expense, effort and time is spent in converting the latter to the former, we could well agree that if source data could be prepared in the equivalent of binary form, i.e. selection or non-selection of pre-determined factors, then we have a medium that having been read can be input direct into a computer. If, for example, we take a question with a multiple choice answer

Is Grass? Green, Yellow, Red, Violet, Blue

then the answer can be given with a stroke of a pen, i.e. crossing through or underlining 'Green'. We then have a Yes—No condition for all of the variables quoted, in other words the question has been answered with, Yes, No, No, No, No. All we need now is a reader which will differentiate between the marked and the unmarked variables and we have a direct computer input in binary terms, using one document only recording data at source and eliminating the intermediary steps converting

1234567890-*.

1234567890-*.

(a)

1234567890

90 ... I: .' II"

1234567890 ... I: .' II"

(b)

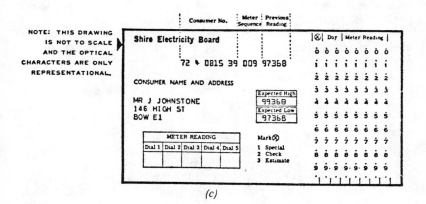

NOTE: THIS DRAWING
IS NOT TO SCALE
AND THE OPTICAL
CHARACTERS ARE ONLY
REPRESENTATIONAL.

(c)

Figure 4.4. (a) An MICR fount
(b) An OCR fount
(c) An OCR mark-sensing document

source data to a computer acceptable form. Naturally the answer key will be held in the program so that comparisons can be made and right or wrong decided.

This system, usually known as *optical mark reading* can be used in many applications in commercial systems. It involves the use of pre-printed forms of sizes within tolerances that are acceptable to the reader, and also the positioning in print of the variables to be compatible with the positioning of the machine's sensing heads.

The technique of source data recording lends itself to a number of commercial procedures such as stock-taking by using printed stock-lists against which are shown a range of stock levels, the appropriate one being marked after a physical stock count.

KEYBOARD DEVICES

This is a rather comprehensive term and strictly speaking can be used in connection with any device into which data is manually inserted through a keyboard. As such it could well include devices for the preparation, for example, of punched cards, punched paper tape, and magnetic tape character encoding.

Within the concept of basic computer input devices, however, we are thinking in terms of those machines which, by manipulation of a keyboard, transmit data direct to the computer store, that is, devices that are 'on-line' to the computer. This type of equipment consists essentially of a keyboard containing not only keys representing characters for recording data, but also keys for conveying instructions relating to the transmission of such data to the computer. The machine incorporates the necessary circuitry to produce the relevant binary pattern for acceptance by the computer (Figure 4.5). By definition, this kind of input is necessarily slow, speed of recording being limited to the rate of key depressions, around a maximum of 300 characters per minute.

With this type of terminal, transmission of data as and when it is keyed-in would indeed lead to very uneconomic use of the computer as the central processor could be tied up over fairly long periods of time working at a rate far below its capacity. To get around this problem a small memory store can be incorporated into the terminal hardware in which data is initially and temporarily stored. When the computer is ready to accept this data it can then be transferred at high speed in bulk. In this way a multiple number of terminals can be linked on-line to the computer, all accepting data simultaneously, and holding it in the buffer store of each terminal. The computer will then search around the terminals, transferring the contents of these buffers into its own store in rotation. Since this search and transfer process is so rapid, each terminal appears to be in direct communication with the computer all the time (Figure 4.6).

Figure 4.5. Computer terminal and keyboard (Westrex Company Ltd.)

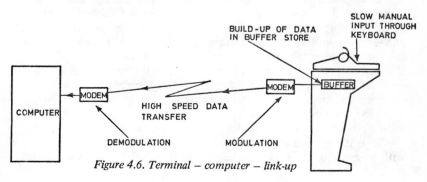

Figure 4.6. Terminal — computer — link-up

FUTURE TRENDS IN INPUT

The main problems found in large scale computer data processing, are the time-consuming, expensive and laborious processes involved in preparing data in a form that can be read by machines and in turn converted into a form that the computer can accept and store. As we have seen, techniques and devices have been and are in the process of being developed that, to a degree, cut down the amount of work involved by eliminating some of the stages in its preparation.

One obvious way of by-passing these data preparation and conversion procedures is in the area of acoustic signals. This is a computer with the capability of hearing and accurately storing in digital form data so communicated. Another way is in reading hand written source data.

A great deal of experimental work is going on to develop voice systems although, of course, the main problem centres around the infinite variety of intonations used by different people in the process of speech. A way around this problem is to train the machine to recognise a limited range of words spoken by one individual person. The user repeats to the machine a number of times the words or phrases to be used. The waveform resulting from each is stored as a pattern and given a digital coding. The computer then, hearing a sound, will compare it with the stored patterns until a match is found and then generate and store the relevant digital code. A simple application of such a system could be in the recording of goods issued in a stock control procedure. A series of numbers would be spoken identifying the quantity issued and the part number of the item, e.g. 25 1472 (spoken Two Five—One Four Seven Two), for direct input to computer storage. In this case the number of recognition patterns stored need be limited to the ten digits only.

Again, developments are proceeding in which movement patterns of a pen used in ordinary writing can be transmitted to a computer and identified in terms of letters. This is a pen with an ordinary ball-point tip to enable a hard copy to be made, but containing small motion transducers that sense the direction of its movement. The wave pattern so produced is compared with standard patterns in its control module and on recognition its appropriate digital coding is stored either on cassette magnetic tape for later reading into the computer, or direct to the computer store in an 'on-line' mode. At the same time a digital read-out is displayed for verification purposes, errors being corrected by erasing an incorrect character by drawing a line through it.

Video systems are also being developed to recognise objects and so enable a computer to record the movement of such objects, precluding the need for written input records. Such a device consists of a camera with an array of small photodiodes upon which an image of the object is projected. It is then scanned to produce a series of analog electrical pulses which vary proportional with the light falling on the diodes. They are then compared with pre-stored patterns and on recognition are converted to the appropriate digital pattern identifying the object.

EXERCISES

1. Describe how data originating in hand-written form can be prepared for entry to a computer.

2. Why do you think, in spite of new developments in computer input, punched cards still remain the most popular medium for recording data to be read into a computer?

3. Describe three methods of capturing data for direct input to a computer.

4. What do you understand by MICR and OCR input media? Mention any major advantage or disadvantage these systems may have.

5. Keyboard terminals present a convenient way of conveying data to a computer and eliminate the need for data conversion processes. In the light of this, discuss the limitations and disadvantages you feel are evident in the use of terminals.

6. Data for computer processing can be captured either 'off-line' or 'on-line'. What do you understand by the term 'Data Capture' and explain the difference in treatment, using examples to illustrate your answer, of data captured in these two ways.

5

Computer Output

This chapter reviews output methods, the factors that determine the method used, and considerations that will determine the mode of such output.

As we have seen from previous chapters, the preparation of data for final input to a computer can be a laborious, expensive and time-consuming affair. Much research and experimentation has gone into trying to simplify data preparation and conversion techniques, mainly with the object of reducing the number of stages through which data has to pass before being received by the central processor.

However, when we consider the output function of a computer it becomes apparent that this is usually a one-stage operation. Although work is constantly proceeding to speed up and improve quality and techniques there is not the scope to cut down the stages involved as with the input of data. In computer output we are mainly concerned with a clear and definitive information statement which, in the final analysis, is humanly interpretable. There are obviously limits to the forms this can take (Figure 5.1).

OUTPUT METHODS

Fundamentally, the output peripherals of a computer can be divided into four groups producing information in these ways:

(a) Printed
(b) Coded
(c) Optical
(d) Diagrammatic

However, this is rather an arbitary division, as some kinds of output device will incorporate more than one of these functions.

Printed output

There are three main types of printing device used in association with computers; line printers; single character printers and optical printers.

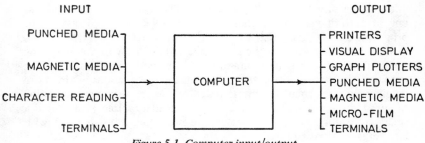

Figure 5.1. Computer input/output

Line printers. As the name suggests, these are machines that print a line of characters virtually simultaneously; there are two main types, barrel and chain printers. On these each print line is built up by one revolution of the barrel or, in the case of a chain printer, a line for each circuit of the chain. In both cases the type faces are continually moving at high speed, and hammers, one for each character position in the print line, strike the surface of the paper imprinting the required characters as they are presented at the print-line position in turn.

For high output volumes of data, as in most commercial data processing systems, line printers are the most popular and generally used form of output for a number of reasons. They are very fast and any modern printer will cope with 1200 lines of 120 characters a minute. They provide a permanent copy of records; carbon interleaved stationary can be used to produce a number of copies simultaneously if required. A finished product is produced; in using pre-printed forms as the top copy, invoices, statements of account, cheques, salary statements etc can be produced ready for immediate despatch.

A number of observations are frequently made centring around the quality of printing produced by this type of printer. One criticism is that type tends to be a little blurred and indistinct. This may be true of a minority of printers but generally speaking, particularly for top copies, the imprint is quite well defined. Another, and possibly more valid point, is that the mass of printing often found on print-outs is dull in presentation and does not adequately highlight salient points in a report.

Part of the fault may well be in the monotony inherent in printing all characters in upper case, although the technical problems involved, both in hardware and software, of developing a line printer that will print in both upper and lower case as fast as present printers, are formidable. Another part of the fault may well find its remedy in more effective editing procedures. Such procedures, designed to give a more attractive layout, could well be at the expense of speed, bearing in mind that a print-line of 10 characters will take as long to produce as one of 120 characters and that, by and large, it will take as long to produce a blank spacing line, as for a line of characters.

One developing area in the use of line printers is, with the increasing use of powerful centralised computers, their employment as terminals, or satellites remote from the main machine. As discussed in more detail in another chapter, remote batch processing terminals consisting of input devices, usually a punched card reader, a line printer and a small controlling central processor, are becoming more popular with large organisations and bureaux.

Single character printers.   These are similar to a typewriter, and print characters in succession one at a time. These devices are normally connected on-line to a computer and may transmit information in both directions, input as we have seen is through keyboard operation, and output automatically printed arising from signals transmitted from the computer. As these devices have a slow transfer rate, use can be made of the ordinary Post Office telephone network, although such lines are unsuitable for conveying high speed transmissions. The normal Post Office dialling system is used to link into the computer, contact being signalled by an audible 'carrier wave' tone. A press of a button will then establish the link in a mode ready for transmission.

Transmission in this way involves the use of an interface between the telephone line and the computer equipment at both ends, terminal and central processor. The device providing this interface is known as a *modem.*

Modem is an abbreviation of 'modulator–demodulator'. Telephone lines used in the Post Office network carry alternating current in the form of analogues, or representations of speech. Each sound generates a wave pattern that is transmitted over the lines and converted back to an audio signal at the other end. Terminal to computer cable links operate by transmitting binary signals, a two state situation, indicating the presence or absence of a particular voltage level. Thus, direct current which permits just these two possible states only must be used for data transmission in this mode.

Modulation is the process of converting the digital data (i.e. data in binary form) to analogue data for transmission, and demodulation is the technique of reversing this process at the computer end. It is therefore necessary to have modems at both ends of the link, Figure 4.6.

However, there is a second way of transmitting data from terminals operating at a slow input output rate. This is accomplished by the use of a device known as an *acoustic coupler* (see Figure 5.2). In this case the telephone instrument itself is inverted into a cradle on the terminal designed for this purpose. The digital signals from the terminal are·

converted into audio signals and these are transmitted over the line in much the same way as speech signals. At the computer end they are converted back to binary pulses ready for entry to the central processor.

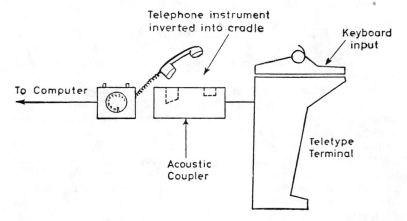

Figure 5.2. Terminal used with acoustic coupler (K & N Electronics Ltd.)

Disadvantages to this mode of data transmission are:

(a) low transmission speed, maximum effective rate is 200 bands (i.e. bits per second), and

(b) the problems of data becoming corrupted by extraneous noise being picked up on the system.

However, this transmission system has one major advantage in that acoustic coupling can be used direct with any normal telephone audio instrument, thus permitting the use of portable terminals. These are much the same as an ordinary free-standing teletype terminal but in a more compact and smaller form contained in a large brief case and easily transportable.

Optical printers. Whilst not widely used, these offer an alternative method of providing a permanent printed data record, although this is a highly sophisticated technical process that does contain hazards that may lead to the loss of output data. It works on a principle of projecting

an image of the output data through a cathode-ray tube on to a re-
volving drum with a light sensitive surface. The image so formed is then
transferred to paper using the same method as in xerographic document
reproduction.

Before leaving this discussion on printers as a computer output
medium, mention should be made of the increasing practice of preparing output documents in a form that can be used for re-entry to
the system. These are sometimes known as 'turn-around' documents.
After suitable annotating they become the input documents for the next
processing cycle.

One commonly used application involves the preparation of a
tear-off remittance advice slip as part of the account sent to a customer. Identifying and quantitative data is printed in machine readable
characters, usually an optical character recognition system. When the
customer returns the slip with payment, the detail is read into the
computer store, updating the customer's account. A second application
also now commonly used, is the printing, at the same time as the
customer's account of a 'mark-sensing' document, as described in
Chapter 4. On this form, consumption of a commodity, say gas or
electricity, is marked when meters are read, and then in turn used as
an input document to convey the data necessary for calculating and
preparing the next account.

Coded output

Coded output infers an output medium that is not immediately
humanly readable, but needs to be subjected to an additional process
to make it so. The two main forms of this type of output in data
processing are recorded in:

> (a) punched form on cards or tape and
> (b) on magnetic media.

In the early days of computers, output on punched cards was a
fairly common practice, but today it is rarely used in commercial
systems. The slow and laborious procedure of interpreting cards through
a mechanical tabulator has now been replaced by the use of fast on-line
printers. By the same token, output in the form of punched paper tape
is far too slow a process for most purposes. Perhaps the main virtue in
this mode of output is the production of machine readable documents,
and applications have been designed in which cards are used for re-entry
purposes similar to the application mentioned above to record the
settlement of accounts.

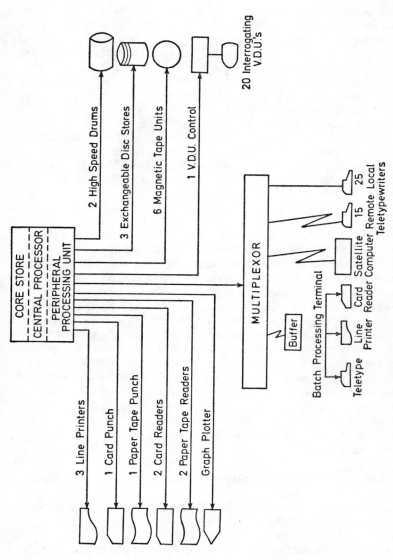

Figure 5.3. Example of medium-sized computer configuration

When considering output to *magnetic media*, it will be appreciated that much of the data resulting from processing is not needed for immediate intelligible communication. The detailed records, for example of issues in a stock control system, may never be required in detailed print form, but nevertheless are an output resulting from processing records of such issues. The purpose of such processing may be purely to produce summarised accounts of stock issues, receipts, current stock levels etc at, say, the end of each month, and it is at that stage that printed records will be prepared.

Indeed we may classify computer output into that output needed to communicate with people, and that to communicate with machines. It is this latter category that is frequently stored in coded form in magnetic media so that it can, in turn, be re-entered easily into the system to produce the ultimate permanent records demanded of the system.

Visual output

This term when associated with computer output is generally taken to mean a display of information on a cathode-ray tube. These devices are known as *visual display units*. Since the main object of this output mode is to enable a user to interrogate records held on computer files, i.e. call up information as and when required, a pre-requisite is the availability of direct access storage. From the user's point of view, the response time, i.e. time between the request for information and its presentation visually, would be far too great if records were stored on a serial access medium—magnetic tape—and a long search was necessary for the records demanded. Another hardware factor to bear in mind is that if a single programming computer is used to output in Visual Display Form, the machine will be standing idle while the user operates the terminal. This type of device should therefore, only be used as a peripheral of a computer with a multi-processing facility so that the machine can carry on other work while the information is being projected onto the VDU.

The main advantages accruing to the use of visual display units are:

(a) the rapid response time, i.e. information presented almost immediately on request,

(b) saving in computer time that would otherwise be occupied in printing out a hard copy, and

(c) saving on supplies, paper etc.

Among disadvantages of the VDU, however, are:

(a) the cost involved, not only of the terminals themselves, but the fairly large configuration necessary to support them,

(b) the complexity of the software necessary for their operation,

(c) that only a temporary record is available that, should it be required in permanent form would involve a further process.

While we are concerned in this chapter with output methods, it is relevant to mention at this point that VDU's are sometimes used in association with keyboard devices for input purposes. Stock balances, for example, can be displayed and updated visually by the insertion of stock receipts through the keyboard.

While, perhaps, it does not truly fall within the category of visual display, output on *microfilm* is a convenient way of permanently recording output data. It also provides a medium through which a hard copy may be obtained when required, as well as incorporating the advantages normally associated with microfilm records such as economy in storage space, and convenience of retrieval. The earlier use of microfilm involved a two-stage process, first producing a hard copy of the output and then photographing it. However, techniques have been developed for transference direct from magnetic tape to microfilm, an extremely fast method of producing a permanent copy. It is interesting to note that the National Giro System uses microfilm for some of its computer output.

Diagrammatic output

It is sometimes desirable to present the output in diagrammatic or graphical form. The two ways of doing this are by the use of a *Digital Increment Plotter* (Figure 5.4) to provide a permanent record or a VDU to provide a temporary visual record. In the former case, data

Figure 5.4. Example of digital increment plotter output

stored in digital form is used to control the movement of a pen and also the drum on which the paper is mounted. This provides the facility for plotting a line in any direction. Relative movement speeds between drum and pen will also gives lines of any curvature.

While not providing a permanent record, a diagrammatic display on a VDU has the advantage that the image can be manipulated, scaled up or down, or even altered in perspective. If required, the electron beam creating the display can be redirected by light pen, automatically modifying the digital data held in store.

Mention should be made of one of the more recent developments in output, that involving the use of voice systems, known as *Acoustic Output*. While voice synthesisers in the form of sophisticated tape or disc recorders have been in use for some time, and it is a comparatively straightforward process to play back selected sounds under computer control, more recent developments involve the storage of sounds, words, etc in digital form in solid state circuitry. These digital signals are read out of store when required, fed through a digital to analogue converter so producing an analogue audio signal for playing through an amplifier to a loudspeaker.

One further form of output that combines a hard copy with a recording on a magnetic medium occurs in the use of *Visible Record Computers* and is dealt with in more detail in Chapter 13.

TYPE OF OUTPUT

In any given situation, the choice of output form will obviously hinge on available peripheral hardware and the power and versatility of the central processor. It is important, therefore, that output requirements be established at the Systems Design Stage so that, either output modes are restricted to the hardware available or that provision is made for the hardware necessary to produce the required output.

Factors that will be taken into consideration when deciding output forms are as follows.

1. The need for a hard copy

If a hard copy is essential, is it required for external or internal distribution? This will determine the quality, and the format of the output and also lead to specifying the need for ancillary equipment to prepare documents for distribution.

The number of copies required must be determined, bearing in mind that a line printer may be expected to produce six reasonable copies. If more are needed, then involving the computer in a second

Output device	Extent of use	Hard copy	External distribution	Interrogation	Permanent file	Intermediate output	Turnaround for re-input	Information retrieval
LINE PRINTER	Extensive	✓	✓		✓		✓	✓
TERMINAL (TYPEWRITER)	Fairly extensive	✓		✓	✓			✓
VISUAL DISPLAY UNIT	Less extensive			✓			✓	✓
GRAPH PLOTTER	Limited	✓	Limited		✓			
MAGNETIC MEDIA	Extensive					✓		
PUNCHED MEDIA	Limited				✓	✓	✓	
MICRO-FILM	Developing (Two-stage)	✓ (Two-stage)	✓ (Second stage)		✓			
AUDIO-RESPONSE	Developing (limited)			✓				✓

Figure 5.5. Use of output devices

print run will be balanced against output in a form that can be readily reproduced off-line, for example, in microfilm form or a print-out of high enough definition for photo-copying or offset-litho printing.

A further consideration is whether the print-out document is needed for re-entry to the system as input. Should this be the case, factors such as paper weight, size, character fount, document layout, will be critical.

2. Response time

If users require information on demand, then some kind of file interrogation system will be necessary, involving direct access to the computer. This could be either in the form of teletype terminals or Visual Display Units. the former having the advantage of giving a hard-copy print-out, but the disadvantage of taking longer to produce the information. A processor with multi-programming facilities will be required to support these terminal devices.

3. Cost

Justification of expenditure will naturally be made within the context of the system objectives. Sufficient perhaps to say that the use on any considerable scale of on-line terminals, visual or teletype, will be more costly both in terms of hardware and software, than conventional line-printer output.

OUTPUT CONTROL

In assuring the adequacy of output to meet user requirements, three areas of control should be increased:

(a) *Control of quality.* This is mainly a question of scrutinising sample output documents to ensure that an acceptable quality of print is being maintained, that no characters are missing, and that the format of the document is correct.
(b) *Quantitative control.* This is mainly concerned with the accurate listing of run totals and their reconciliation with previously established control totals to ensure the arithmetic accuracy of a process.
(c) *Security controls.* In some cases it is essential to account for every sheet of stationery used, as for example, the printing of cheques by computers. In such cases documents are normally numbered serially and a record kept of the range of serial numbers for each run, account also being made of any such forms wasted in the printing process.

One further important point in connection with the control of output centres around the treatment of error reports. Special care must be taken to ensure that necessary action is taken, whether this be of an internal nature, that is, within the data processing department itself, or external, involving reference back to the user.

Finally, we must remind ourselves that, as in the case of input we were concerned with people and machines communicating with a computer, so in output we are concerned with the computer communicating with people and machines. Such information output from the computer may be needed:

(a) For short term action, i.e. decision making or notification of a current situation, for example, a statement of account, an invoice, or a stock level statement.
(b) For long term purposes, for example, records of past transactions that may be required for audit purposes, or records needed over a period of time for reference purposes, such as price lists or lists of Creditor balances.
(c) For re-entry purposes as input data to further processing.

The choice of output medium could well be determined by these three factors. Records for short term action being in hard copy printed form or projected on a Visual Display Unit, the urgency of the requirements dictating whether a line printer with a slow response time or a terminal with a fast response time is used. In category (b) it is usual to, eventually, print out this information either through a line printer or in microfilm form for filing, while data in category (c) would normally involve machine to machine communication; the output stored on magnetic tape or disc for convenient reprocessing when required.

EXERCISES
1. List the main kinds of output device that are used in a commercial data processing situation and in each case give one example of an application in which you feel the device could be used to advantage.

2. Differentiate between a line printer and a single character serial printer. Give examples of the systems context in which these two machines are likely to be used.

3. What do you understand by an 'audio coupler'? Describe how this device is used.

4. What do you understand by a 'turn-around' document? Give a description of an application that makes use of this principle.

5. Give an account of the factors you would take into consideration if you were faced with the choice of using either tele-type terminals or visual display units.

6

Central Processors

In the early days computers were often referred to by the rather fanciful title 'electronic brain'. Today we have come to recognise the limitations of a computer compared with the most important brain function, that of rational creative thinking; this term is seldom used.

However, figuratively speaking it would be realistic to refer to the central processing unit of a computer configuration as the brain of the system, since embodied in this unit is the direction, the control and the essential processing functions, essential for the tasks required of it. The analogy is perhaps further strengthened as we reflect that the functions of our mind include the ability to recognise and accept data, to store it for a period of time, either short-term or long-term, depending on how important the information is to us or how great an impact is has made.

We are also able to manipulate data stored, for example, to compare it with other items of data and so arrive at a decision, or perform arithmetic processes to arrive at a required solution or answer. Not only are we able to store, or remember, information relating to many things and consciously recall it when required, but also to store methods or instructions for dealing with such information and, indeed, modify and short circuit such instructions as the immediate occasion demands. Having arrived at a solution, an answer or a decision, our mind, if we so desire, is then able to output it in one form or another.

One could pursue this comparison a little further by suggesting that our brain is supported by, and controls, a number of other organs and functions. Some of these will accept and transfer information to our brain, as is the case when we hear and see, although the power of our brain to recognise and act on such information will depend on whether it falls outside the limits of what it has learned or been instructed to understand. For example to most of us, reading a book in Chinese or indeed listening to a speech in Chinese, the ideas conveyed would be meaningless because they are unrecognisable. By the same token, some organs and functions will accept information from our brain and communicate it in one form or another to factors outside ourselves.

Thus, perhaps, we have a basic concept of a computer configuration with the central processor, performing functions something like our brain, with peripheral units. Some of these peripheral units are capable of accepting information and transferring it to this central unit, and others capable of accepting information from it and in turn communicating it in understandable form.

However, the analogy must end here. There are limitations in our mental processes that are not found in a computer and conversely, the computer has limitations that are not evident in our own thinking. Within the first category, limitations will include:

(a) *Speed of operation.* A computer is able to accept information, process it and output the results faster than the human brain. When compared with the speed of our own reflex actions, the computer is virtually instantaneous.

(b) *Storing information.* The capacity of a computer to hold information in store is virtually limitless, while we know from experience the limits we experience in our own memory.

(c) *Recalling information.* Whereas a computer, given the appropriate form of storage, can retrieve any item of information in a fraction of a second, we know that some items stored in the recesses of our mind take very much longer than this to recall.

(d) *Complexity of operation.* While we all possess, in varying degrees, the ability to solve problems of both a tactical and mathematical nature, we would all agree that there is a limit to the complexity of problems we can solve without recourse to outside aids of some kind. However complex a problem, providing it is soluble and all the relevant information is to hand, a computer will be able to cope with it.

Among limitations in computer processing are:

(a) *Pure creative thinking.* A computer is able to compare and indeed associate factors, draw conclusions from this and indeed modify factors stored in the light of these conclusions and repeat the process. In this sense although it can be said to create ideas, the computer has in itself, no pure creative ability in the sense of the 'inspiration' we ourselves experience.

(b) *Range of input method.* It is unlikely that computers will ever be developed capable of accepting the range of stimuli and impressions that are capable of conveying information to our brain.

(c) *Range of output method.* A computer can output information in some ways that are beyond the scope of human beings, for example, a computer projection on a cathode ray tube. However, conveying information by a glance, touch or indeed by a movement are beyond the capabilities of a computer.

(d) *Modifying decisions.* There are some, purely subjective factors that we, in our thinking, are able to take into account in arriving at decisions, for example, the effect of the decision on a specific person. There are also considerations of conscience, ideology and motive that a computer is unable to take fully into account.

BASIC CENTRAL PROCESSOR FUNCTIONS

In essence, we can summarise the basic functions common to all computer central processors as follows; although as we shall see later, the complexity and the power of some of these functions will vary from computer to computer (Figure 6.1).

(a) Storage of program instructions.
(b) Execution of program instructions.
(c) Storage of data.
(d) Transference of data to and from itself to peripheral devices, and to varying positions within itself.
(e) Arithmetic processes.
(f) Control instructions to govern the operation of the whole configuration.

Before considering these functions individually, let us first review general ideas on storage in a central processor.

Basic principles of storage

The basic indivisible unit of storage is a binary bit, and the mechanics of its storage is a device which can physically be in one of two states. An electric light bulb is an example of this principle in that it can be either 'on' or 'off'. While a number of different types of device are available which will conform with this principle, the most commonly used in central processors at the moment is a small ferrite ring which is capable of being magnetised in either of two directions, clockwise or anti-clockwise.

If we suggest that a field flowing in a clockwise direction represents a binary zero, while in an anti-clockwise direction a binary one, then we have a medium for recording data in binary form. Furthermore, if when an electric current of a critical amplitude is passed through the centre of the ring in one direction, the polarity of the magnetism is

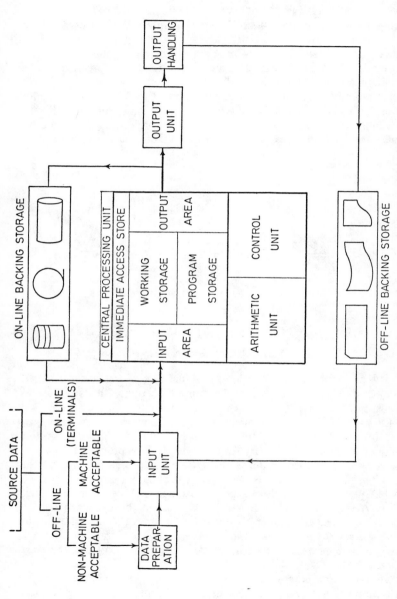

Figure 6.1. Basic functions of computer and inter-relation

reversed, but if it is passed in the opposite direction the polarity remains stable, then we have the means of recording binary digits at will. Taking this a stage further, if after the passage of the electric pulses the ring still retains permanently a residue of the magnetism induced, then we have a device that will retain over a period of time the representation of the digits we wish to hold in store, Figure 6.2.

An assembly containing a large number of these rings, accessible by wires that will convey to any individually selected ring a current sufficient to change its state, gives us the capacity to store quantities of data in binary form. This process is known as writing information to store.

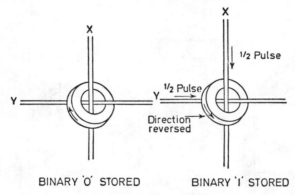

Figure 6.2. Ferrite ring core store

The problem of reaching each individual ring with a pulse sufficient to alter its state is achieved by bisecting each ring with two wires, as shown in Figure 6.3, each carrying half of the current necessary so that at the point of intersection a current of sufficient amplitude is present.

Naturally, having stored information in the central processor in this way, we must have the facility for retrieving it. This process is known as 'Reading from the Computer Store'. The method used is based on the principle that if a current is applied to the ring in a direction that will change its state, then this change of state will itself produce an electric pulse. A third wire, a sensing wire, is threaded through each ring on which this pulse can be picked up so that a series of pulses are output from the sensing wire, representing those rings whose state are changed, thus giving a representation of the data originally stored in the rings (Figure 6.4).

Of course, on completion of this process, all the rings so read will be in a common state, a process sometimes known as 'Zeroising'. It may

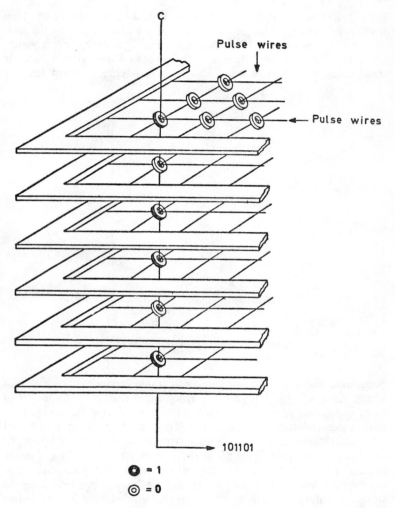

Figure 6.3. Section of core store

well be that the data read out needs to be retained for future processing, in which case the current in the sensing wire can be amplified, redirected to the rings through the two 'write' wires, and so re-establish the original state of the rings.

Having reviewed, in principle, how data in binary form is written to and read from ferrite core store, it will be appreciated that a mass of such devices recording the equivalent of 0's and 1's is meaningless unless organised in some understandable way. In the same way that the mass of characters we use in writing are organised into groups known as words, the bits in a computer store are also organised into groups, also, in most cases known as 'words'. The main difference between the two

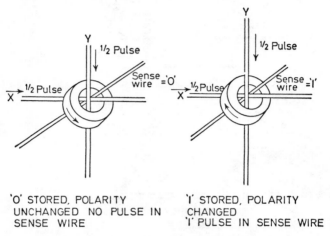

'O' STORED, POLARITY
UNCHANGED NO PULSE IN
SENSE WIRE

'I' STORED, POLARITY
CHANGED
'I' PULSE IN SENSE WIRE

Figure 6.4. Reading operation from core store

being that whereas in writing the considerable variance in the length of words can easily be defined by leaving a space, or gap, at the end of each, in a computer store this is impractical. A solution lies in standard-ising a computer 'word' length by giving each the same number of bits. This standard length will vary from machine to machine, some machines having a word length of say 12 bits, another of 24 and so on. So, a storage unit is a defined number of ferrite cores each capable of representing one binary bit, in which one binary expression can be stored, the standard number of bits in the word (Figure 3.1) providing the mechanics of distinguishing one expression from another.

In order to locate any specific item of information it is, of course, necessary to know in which of the many words contained in the com-puter store, the relevant item is held. This is done by giving each word a unique reference, or 'Address'. Whilst, in the early days of computers, it was necessary for the programmers to keep an index of address references against the data item stored, all machines, nowadays, keep in the central processor their own index system so that reference to any data item by program or operator will be automatically traced to its correct location or address.

In Chapter 3 'Computer Arithmetic', the number of bit places necessary to record a given expression were reviewed. These group sizes are not necessarily compatible with the standard word length in the computer store. For instance, a standard word length of 24 bits provides far more capacity than is needed to store the binary equivalent of the decimal digit 9, that is 1001 in binary. While this 24-bit word may be very convenient for storing large numbers in pure binary, or indeed numbers that need to be expressed to a high degree of accuracy in binary fraction, it is not economic for the small groupings required for storing alphabetical characters or numbers in binary coded decimal, binary coded octal or binary coded hexadecimal form. For coping with these, perhaps the obvious thing to do is to divide the 24 bit word up into a number of sub-groups, each containing say four bits, and use each of these small groups to represent one digit. To enable us to distinguish alphabet from numeric characters two groups can be used to represent a character other than a digit.

Having seen how data is, in principle, held in the central processor store, let us look a little more closely at the basic processor functions listed earlier in this chapter. It must be remembered that there is no standard storage format common to all makes of machines; word lengths and the organisation and definition of data in store will vary from machine to machine.

Storage of program instructions

The basic purpose of a computer is to execute the instructions, previously determined through a systems design procedure, converted to operational instructions by a programmer, and then stored in the computer processor. Indeed, it is this capacity to store instructions, execute them, and then on its own decision to repeat the process until the machine itself, acting on prescribed criteria decides to stop, all without operator intervention, that is perhaps the most important distinguishing feature in a computer compared with other calculating and data processing devices.

Even the simplest instructions used in everyday life must contain two elements to make them capable of intelligent execution. One element specifies the action to be taken and the other the medium on which the action is to be performed. The first of these two elements is called the *Operation* and the second, the *Operand*. For instance, in the instruction 'read a book', the operation element is to read, and the operand, the book. However, if access to a specific passage in the book is required, the operand in this instruction is insufficiently defined, the location of the passage would need to be specified, i.e. 'read line 24 on page 129 of this book'. Obviously, in processing data by computer, this principle of positively identifying the data required must be observed. As we saw earlier, data items are held in store in words, each word having a unique address. So, to identify the data, all that is necessary is to quote the operational address, or addresses at which the data is stored.

By definition, there will be a limit to the number of functions any device or machine will perform. Since this number is finite it is a quite straight-forward procedure to allocate each a code number and to use this code to communicate the operation to the machine. This list of codes representing computer functions, or the operation element of the program instructions is known as a *machine code*.

With different machines, the format of the instruction will vary, while at the same time retaining in principle an operation and an operand. The instruction may specify the function code and one address only, i.e. an instruction to do something with the data stored in that address, this is known as a *single address* instruction. A *two-address* instruction will, as the name implies, specify in some systems the address of the operand and the address of the next instruction, or in other systems, an address in which the results of processing are to be stored rather than the next instruction address. *Three-* and *four-address* systems will contain, in addition to the operation code, the address of the next instruction and the addresses of two or three data locations. In the four-address instruction one of these locations will be the designated location of the result of processing arising from the interaction of the other two items of data.

The more elements an address format contains, the more uneconomic in terms of storage space it is likely to be. To use a four-address format for an instruction needing only the function code and a single data address would waste three of the five words comprising the format. The most widely used address in computers today is the two instruction format. It should be noted that instruction formats, while they vary from machine to machine, are fixed for any particular machine.

Program instructions are held in words in store in the same way as data items. It is not usual to segregate a part of the store for this purpose, but all words can be used for storing either data or instructions. However, they must be stored in such a way that each instruction will automatically generate access to the next instruction in sequence. If they are stored in consecutive word locations, then the control function need only access them in turn. However, should there be a gap in addresses between one and the next instruction to be executed, the former will have to quote the address of the latter.

Execution of program instructions

While detailed techniques for moving and accessing data in the processor will vary from machine to machine, the essential steps in executing an instruction are as follows (Figure 6.5):

(a) Location of the first instruction to be carried out and its transference to a control unit.
(b) Extraction from store of the data to be worked on, the address of which is specified in the operand element of the instructions.
(c) Carrying out the operation specified in the instructions on the data in (b) above.
(d) Location of next instruction and a repetition of the above sequence.

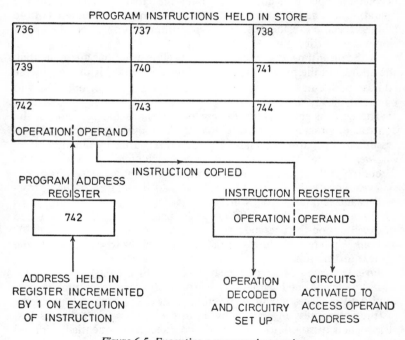

Figure 6.5. Executing a program instruction

While a detailed technical description of how these stages are carried out is not the province of this book, the following comments seek to give a fairly simple explanation of the process.

It will be appreciated that the first instruction to be executed may be stored in any location in the central processor, and it cannot be identified until the address of this location is specified. The first stage is to communicate the address of this first instruction which may be done by operator intervention or specified in the program. The address is entered into a control register, usually known as a program register; this will now control each step until the cycle of operations for executing the instruction is complete.

Reference is now made to the address stored in the program register, through the medium of an address selector, and the instruction contained in this is read out to another register known as an instruction register. This register now contains both elements of the instruction, the operand address and the operation code. The next steps are to decode the operation code in terms of the circuitry to carry out the operation, i.e. add, subtract, shift etc and to move the contents of the address specified in the operand to an arithmetic unit where the operation will be carried out.

In the meantime, assuming in this case all instructions are sequential, the address in the program register will be updated by 1, thus giving the address of the next instruction so enabling this cycle of operations to be automatically repeated.

The control and timing of these operations is the function of the control, or program register, which, by keeping in step with the processor's timing patterns will, in effect, do this routine by numbers

One. Locate instruction in storage by reference to the program control register and transfer it to the instruction register.

Two. Locate the operand by reference to the address in the instruction and remove it from storage.

Three. Decode the operation code part of the instruction and execute it on the operand.

Four. Update the address in the control register to give access to the next instruction.

Five. Go back to one and repeat the cycle (Figure 6.6).

It was mentioned earlier that in order to provide automatic continuity to a succession of instructions it was necessary to update the instruction address in control by 1; this, of course, pre-supposes that all program instructions are stored and executed sequentially. Indeed the only way a computer can follow through a series of instructions is, having been informed of the address of the first, to work through consecutive addresses until it is told to do otherwise. As is often the case, should it be necessary to break this chain of consecutive addresses, then the instruction in the last of the one series must be used to direct control to the first of the new (Figure 6.7).

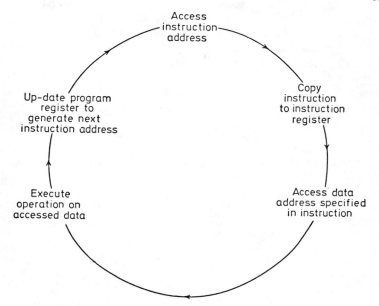

Figure 6.6. Execution cycle of program instruction

ADDRESS

11250	11251	11252	11253	11254	11255
DATA	DATA	DATA	PROGRAM	PROGRAM	PROGRAM
11256	11257	11258	11259	11260	11261
PROGRAM	PROGRAM	PROGRAM	PROGRAM	DATA	DATA
11262	11263	11264	11265	11266	11267
DATA	DATA	DATA	DATA	DATA	DATA
11268	11269	11270	11271	11272	11273
DATA	PROGRAM	PROGRAM	PROGRAM	PROGRAM	PROGRAM

Program instructions are worked sequentially from word 11253.
Word 11259 contains a jump instruction directing control to word 11269.

Figure 6.7. Store location with program instruction

We have already noted that perhaps the main distinguishing feature of a computer compared with other data processing devices, is its ability to repeat indefinitely a series of instructions, and to apply them to variable data, without operator intervention. While, for a specific computer run, the program will only be completed once in its entirety, nevertheless, within the program will be groups of instructions that have to be repeated over and over again, these groups are usually known as *Program Loops*.

For example, in a program designed to prepare invoices, the data for preparing the cost of the items may only consist of part numbers associated with quantity delivered. In this case, for every line entry on the invoice, the computer may have to locate the part description and part unit cost, multiply the unit cost by quantity and record the resulting answer. This process will have to be completed for every item listed on the invoice, thus the instructions to complete this process are repeated until the invoice is complete. Entry into the loop in these circumstances is implemented by what is known as a *Branch Instruction*.

Since the addresses of the instructions comprising the loop remain constant, the final instruction must direct control back to the first to enable the cycle to be repeated. However, if this is an unqualified direction the machine would keep working through the loop indefinitely. A way, therefore, must be provided to break out of the loop when appropriate.

The process of breaking out of a loop is accomplished by the use of what is known as a *Conditional Branch Instruction,* although there are many situations in which this type of instruction is employed other than terminating a loop. In fact, this instruction, sometimes also known as a *Conditional Jump,* is used whenever a decision has to be taken by the machine, the result of which will involve alternative courses of action.

In the above example a separate invoice must be prepared for each customer, and it is necessary to know where the list of items supplied to one customer ends and the next begins. This can be done by associating a customer reference number with each item and instructing the computer to compare each reference number with the preceding one. If it is the same, the machine will re-enter the loop repeating the above routine, but if different, will be directed to a completely different set of instructions, say calculating a total for all items on the invoice (Figure 6.8).

Finally, there are standard routines which may be called for in any program, but to write these into every program using them would create a lot of unnecessary programming work. These standard routines are known as *Sub-routines* and are frequently supplied in package form by the manufacturers. Examples include sub-routines for sorting,

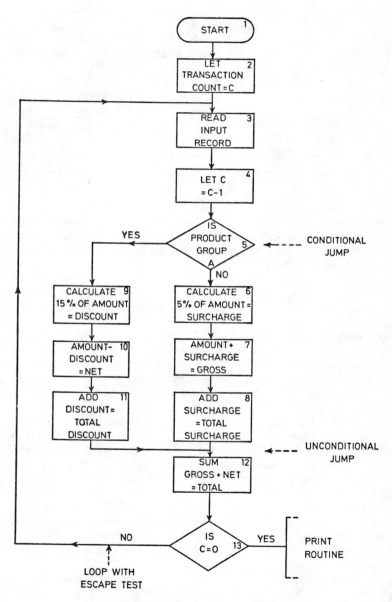

Figure 6.8. Flow chart illustrating jumps

calculating square routes, loading data or programs into store and output routines for writing to tape, print etc.

These sub-routines may be held in on-line backing storage and called into the central processor by the main program as required, or the

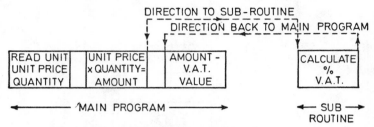

Figure 6.9. Treatment of sub-routines

required sub-routines may be fed into the central processor with the main program at the commencement of a run. In either case the main program will contain instructions to call in the sub-routine when its use is required (Figure 6.9).

Storage and movement of data

Within the computer configuration data may be stored in three basic ways:

(a) In the central processor store.

(b) In on-line backing storage devices such as magnetic tape and magnetic discs.

(c) Off-line on media that can be easily stored in a library i.e. reels of magnetic tape and exchangeable disc packs, that can be loaded on-line as required.

The above does not discount data that is stored in punched card, punch tape, or optical character form. These are usually regarded as intermediate forms of storage, that is data which is in the course of transference from source document stage to storage in (a), (b) or (c) above. It is not usual, nowadays, to keep large data files in card or tape form.

An important point to bear in mind is the vast difference in working speed between the central processor which will cope with, say, 1 000 000 calculations a second, and the speed of input and output peripherals transferring data at only a few thousand characters a second. This means that the working efficiency of the processor will be increased as the transfer of data to and from it is speeded up. If we can get the processor to work on the other tasks while it is waiting for data, then it's efficiency will be materially increased.

The factors that need to be present in the processor for processing to take place are:
1. Program instructions.
2. Data upon which the instructions are to work.
3. Control mechanism to time and govern the operating cycle.
4. An operating system to control the activities of the whole configuration.

We have seen how instructions are stored and how access is made to data from the addresses quoted in each instruction. In data processing it is impractical to hold all the data relating to a given procedure or system in the processor's store at one time; this would involve such a large store that the cost would be prohibitive. The practice is, therefore, to hold bulk data in backing storage, usually magnetic disc or tape, and read into the processor blocks of this bulk data as and when required. As we shall see in the next chapter on Storage, access to information in backing store will differ with the type of store, as will indeed the volume of data transferred at any one time.

EXERCISES

1. Give a short account of the main functions of a Central Processing Unit.

2. Describe how the storage of information is organised in the store of the central processor.

3. Describe briefly the routine for executing program instructions in the computer processor.

4. What do you understand by a program 'Jump'. Give examples of the two types of jump.

5. A central processor store will usually hold only a fraction of the total data associated with a data processing system. Explain how the computer deals with the processing of all the records involved.

6. What are the characteristics that distinguish a computer from other forms of calculating device?

7

Computer Storage

The purpose of this chapter is to review the different types of storage media used in computers, to compare their properties and to discuss their relevance to varying processing modes and systems. It is usual to classify storage media under two main types, these are known as immediate access storage, and backing storage. The former, IAS, refers to that storage which forms an integral part of the central processor and holds both the program and the data required for immediate processing. In most machines today this is the ferrite core type of store, although, as we shall see later, a great deal of research is going on into developing other types of store that have this immediate access capability. However, core stores have been dealt with in some detail in Chapter 6, so this chapter will concentrate mainly on backing stores.

The essential difference between backing storage and immediate access storage is, as the names suggest, one of speed and convenience of retrieval, that is locating the particular item of stored data we require. The facts which are constantly needed in everyday life are stored in different ways. Some, a small minority, are stored in our brain, but a large proportion are stored in media external to ourselves, i.e. books, pictures, records etc. Generally speaking, access to those facts stored in our brain is far quicker and indeed more convenient than the sometimes rather laborious procedure of looking them up in dictionaries, encyclopaedias and the like. Our brain is an immediate access type of storage and the other media are types of backing storage.

First of all, to review briefly the different kinds of backing store commonly used in computers. These are:

Magnetic tapes;
Magnetic drums;
Magnetic discs;
Magnetic cards;
Magnetic strips;
Magnetic stripes.

The nature of the physical construction of these types of store will determine how individual items of data can be located. To find an item stored on magnetic tape it is necessary to run the tape over a reading head until the item sought is located. Magnetic drums and discs have the whole recording surface accessible at any one time providing a means of going direct to any specific item of data, while magnetic cards and strips can be individually selected from a magazine at will and so provide a means of directly accessing the data recorded on them.

In the storage media listed above, magnetic tape is known as serial access storage, while the other four are, to a greater or lesser degree, direct access storage.

MAGNETIC TAPE

1. Physical characteristics

Most magnetic tape used in computer storage is ½ in wide and made of a tough plastic such as Mylar. It is coated with a material that can be permanently magnetised and is held on spools of varying lengths, up to 2400 ft.

Tape is processed on an 'on-line' peripheral device known as a tape transport. Depending on central processor hardware, a number of transports can be linked to the processor at the same time. On the transport, the tape is fed from a feed reel to a take-up reel over read and write heads; some transports have an additional erase head, although in many cases the write head serves a dual purpose; to write and erase.

2. Mode of recording

Individual characters are recorded as a line of small areas or dots across the width of the tape representing binary bits, magnetised in the opposite direction to the permanent field on the tape. The positioning of bits longitudinally on the tape are on what are known as 'tracks'.

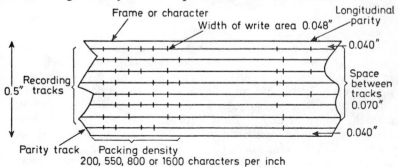

Figure 7.1. Section of magnetic tape

Tape will usually carry 7 or 9 tracks, one of which is used for parity purposes leaving 6 or 8 tracks to record the bit pattern representing the character (Figure 7.1).

The number of characters recorded in a given length of tape is known as the 'packing density' and varies from system to system. It is expressed in terms of characters per inch of tape and common packing densities are 200, 550, 800 and 1600. Information is written to and read from the tape through the central processor store. This may involve reading from one tape and writing to a second, or the use of another type of input or output peripheral in conjunction with the tape. For example, reading may be from punched cards with writing to tape or reading from tape to output on a line printer.

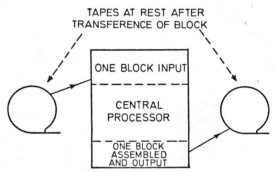

Figure 7.2. Magnetic tape. Movement to and from CPU store

Since data must be moved from the input peripheral to the computer store and then in turn transferred to the output device, the size of available core store will determine the amount of data that can be so moved at one time (Figure 7.2).

3. Organisation of data

A continuous succession of rows of bits representing characters on tape would obviously in itself be meaningless, the limits of each group representing a data field must be defined and in turn the range of fields making up a data record must be indicated. This is done by inserting markers; that is, a special pattern of bits the computer will recognise as such, known as End of Field Markers (EFM) and End of Record Markers (ERM). As mentioned earlier, it is impractical to move data continuously from tape to central processor store because of limitations in its available storage space. It is necessary therefore to break down the information on the tape into segments of a convenient size that the computer can digest one at a time. These segments are known as data blocks. Each block contains one or more complete data records, and the size of the block is defined by an End of Block Marker, in the same way as are fields and records.

Given this principle of transferring data in blocks then the tape itself, instead of moving at a continuous even speed will be required to move in short bursts, starting at the beginning and stopping at the

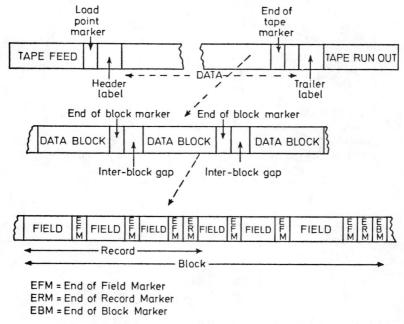

EFM = End of Field Marker
ERM = End of Record Marker
EBM = End of Block Marker

Figure 7.3. Layout on tape markers and inter-block gaps

end of each block. Since reading and writing takes place at a critical speed of tape movement, an unrecorded length of tape must be left between blocks to enable the tape to come to a stop and then pick up speed again. This space is known as an Inter-Block Gap (Figure 7.3).

Data blocks need not be of a fixed length or indeed contain a standard number of records. Systems considerations will determine whether a variable or Fixed Length Block mode of recording is used, bearing in mind, however, that blocks will have both a critical minimum and maximum length determined by hardware considerations.

Taking a magnetic tape as a whole, it will contain the following elements:

(a) A length of tape about 10 ft long to thread from the feed spool, through the deck's mechanism to the take-up spool.
(b) *A load point marker.* This is a light reflecting strip across the width of the tape to indicate to the machine the point at which recording can commence.
(c) *A header label.* This occupies the first recording block and contains identification and control information.
  1. A code identifying the block as a header label.
  2. Tape serial number.
  3. File identification by name, reel number within the file and generation number.
  4. Retention period, after which date the file can be scratched.
  5. Date written.
  6. Space for engineer's use.
  7. Control software.
(d) Inter-block gaps alternating with
(e) Recording blocks which may hold data or, in the case of a program held on tape, program instructions.
(f) The final block on the tape is known as a trailer label containing identification and control information.
  1. A code identifying the block as a trailer label.
  2. File control information specifying whether end of file or referring to file continuation tape.
  3. Data block count.
  4. Control software.
(g) An End of Tape Marker. This is another light reflecting strip across the width of the tape to indicate the point at which the final block can be recorded.
(h) A length of tape, about 12 ft long, for threading up purposes.

5. Read and write operations
Recording, or writing data to tape, is initiated by a program instruction which will specify the location of the data in store to be transferred to tape and also the tape deck holding the tape to which the data is to be written. The 'write' head over which the tape travels is then switched on and the tape set in motion.

Any signals on that section of the tape used in the acceleration process are automatically erased, and when the tape reaches the critical speed the control unit accepts signals from the computer store, recording them one character at a time and adding, where necessary, a parity bit to make the total number of bits in each character an odd number. While writing, a longitudinal count is made of the bits in each track and on completion of a block, where the count is an odd number an additional bit is added to give an even parity. A small gap is usually left between the last character and the frame of parity bits.

On the processor generating through the program a 'read' instruction, again the location in store to which data is to be transferred is identified as well as the tape deck holding the tape to be read. One block of data is transferred at a time, the tape coming to rest in the inter-block gap between each read instruction.

Read and write checks are incorporated into tape systems although the mechanics of the checks tend to vary from system to system. However, it is usual to make parity checks both of characters and tracks and many systems incorporate an 'Echo Check'. This is a second reading of each character or a read after write check and the two compared for discrepancies.

Other read and write functions on a tape system include a rewind facility to wind the tape back onto the original feed reel, and the ability to 'back space' one block at a time. Should the read and write checks mentioned above, indicate a fault in the process, this enables a second attempt to be made. Some tape systems incorporate a 'read-reverse' function, which simply means that data can be read when the tape is moving from the take-up reel to the feed reel.

6. Operation speeds and capacity

Two main factors will govern the transfer rate of data to and from magnetic tape. These are
(a) The packing density and
(b) the speed of tape movement over read and write heads.

This transfer rate is expressed in thousands of characters per second, abbreviated as k ch/s. For example, the theoretical transfer rate of a tape moving at 120 inches a second with a packing density of 800 cpi is 96 k ch/s, but of course the average transfer rate for the whole tape will be considerably less because of the time spent in stop/start operations at inter-block gaps.

As tape systems vary widely in packing density and tape speed, it is impractical to give a standard transfer rate; this will, in fact, vary from 10 k ch/s up to 320 k ch/s, in the most technically up-to-date systems. Probably a fair average for the bulk of the systems used in commercial data processing is about 150-200 k ch/s.

The criteria which determine the total recording capacity of a given length reel of tape are again the packing density and considerations of file design such as use of variable or fixed field and record lengths, size of data blocks and the frequency of inter-block gaps. Again, to quote a 'standard' for say a 2400 ft tape is impractical, but with a packing density of 800 cpi it could well be in the neighbourhood of 20 million characters, although in practice in many systems applications it would probably be appreciably lower than this.

7. Systems considerations

As magnetic tape is one continuous length, it is impractical to conveniently select any record required at random. It would be necessary to read the records on the tape serially until the required record was located, which is a lengthy and laborious process. Magnetic tape is therefore used in the context of systems and procedures designed for processing in serial mode.

Each data record is identified by a unique reference known as the record key, and records are organised on the tape in record key sequence. Data to be processed against the tape is presorted into the same sequence, so that for processing purposes the two sets of data can be read in the same order. Given that this principle of sequential access is observed on tape, it can be a very fast and economical processing medium, when compared with some direct access storage modes. Tape is also a convenient medium for program storage with configurations using one program at a time, but is not suitable for machines with a multi-programming facility.

MAGNETIC DISCS

In the early days of the introduction of magnetic storage media, magnetic tape was almost exclusively used; but the inherent problems in the rapid retrieval of records at random, led to the development of media which permitted access to any particular record at will. From these developments came magnetic disc storage which is now widely used. In contrast to the sequential or serial nature of access to magnetic tape, this type of media is known as direct access or random access storage.

The detailed design of disc storage units varies from manufacturer to manufacturer, although having in common the basic principles involved in recording and retrieving data. This section does not set out to describe any particular unit but to illustrate the basic concepts behind this kind of storage.

1. Physical characteristics

The basic recording medium is a disc, coated with a magnetic substance that can be used to store data in bit form on the same principle as magnetic tape. Whereas in tape, the recording tracks run down the length of the tape, on a disc they take the form of a number of concentric circles, divided up into sectors by a number of non-recording lines set as radii from the centre of the disc to its circumference. Transfer of information to and from the disc is through a read/write head mounted on a moveable arm which is able to locate any required

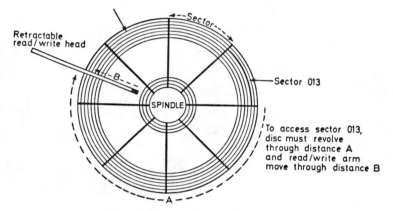

Figure 7.4. Disc showing retractable arm

track on demand. The disc rotates at high speed in relation to the arm, bringing every sector in the located track to the head in turn. Thus a combination of the lateral movement of the read/write head and the circular movement of the disc will provide access to any sector on the surface of the disc (Figure 7.4).

Two distinct types of disc storage are commonly in use, one known as a fixed disc system, has discs mounted permanently in the transport. The other type, an exchangeable disc system, uses packs, or cartridges of discs which, as the name suggests, can be loaded on and off the transport as required.

Fixed Disc Stores.   This usually consists of one or more large discs. Different sized discs are available ranging between 25 and 39 in dia, mounted vertically on a horizontal spindle, rotating at high speed, say 1800 r.p.m. under read/write heads. Due to the size of the disc, the time taken for the head to move through the distance necessary to locate a specific track (known as the 'seek time') is quite high. To reduce this time, many systems incorporate a number of heads on each arm thus limiting the distance over which they travel. Indeed some disc systems use one head per track fixed permanently over the disc surface eliminating completely the time element in locating tracks.

Two major advantages are evident in fixed disc systems compared with exchangeable discs. Firstly, they provide a massive on-line storage capacity. Units are available that will hold up to 600 million characters, and a number of such units can be simultaneously linked to the central processor. The second advantage is that the access time can be much

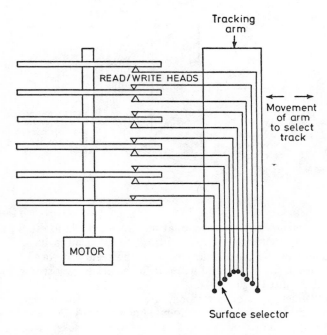

Figure 7.5. Disc pack showing track and surface selection

faster than exchangeable disc packs. This is the case in systems that use a multiple number of heads per surface, so reducing the seek time and where one fixed head per track is used; access time to any sector is reduced to the time taken for the disc to revolve through that distance necessary to bring the sector under the head. This time is known as 'rotational delay'. Access times are in the region of 20 to 25 milliseconds.

Exchangeable Disc Stores.   A similar principle is employed as in the case of magnetic tape where reels of tape can be selected and loaded at will on to a tape deck. Instead of a tape, the recording medium consists of a number of discs mounted on a central spindle, known as a 'disc-pack' or a 'disc-cartridge', the whole of which can be loaded onto or removed from a unit known as a 'disc transport', which is connected on-line to the computer.

When not mounted on the transport, disc packs are housed in transportable plastic containers and can be stored remote from the processor until required for use. When needed, the base of the container is unscrewed, the pack, complete with its top cover, lowered

Figure 7.6. An exchangeable disc pack (IBM Ltd)

onto the drive spindle of the transport, and as the disc pack locks into position the cover is removed, leaving the discs available for use (Figure 7.6).

The discs themselves are somewhat smaller than fixed discs, around 14 in dia. While the number of discs in a pack vary with the manufacturer, the most popular is a pack containing six discs. As with a fixed disc, data is recorded in concentric tracks on the disc surface, each track being divided into a number of sectors separated by inter-block gaps. In a 6-disc pack, only ten surfaces are used for recording purposes, the exposed top and bottom surfaces not being used. It is usual to have only one read/write head per surface, these being mounted on opposite sides of an arm capable of being moved between discs as they rotate on the transport (Figure 7.5).

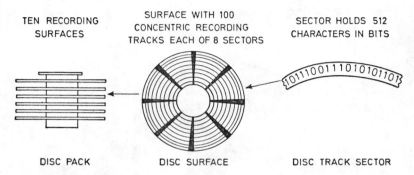

Figure 7.7. Schematic disc pack with arms. Disc surface

In view of the wide range of different disc systems in use it is impractical to quote firm recording capacities and read/write speeds. The number of recording tracks per disc varies between 100 and 200. The recording capacity of all tracks, and indeed, all sectors, is constant in any one disc system, but packing density tends to vary from system to system. It may be as low as 250 or as high as 3000 bits per inch. A fair average in an exchangeable disc system is around 1000. However, it will be appreciated that for any one disc, since the physical length of a track on the perimeter will be greater than one at the centre, the packing density will vary with the position of the track.

Transfer rates are usually within the range 200-350 k ch/s. Access time is represented by the time taken for the head to locate the correct track (seek time), and for the disc to rotate until the address sought is located beneath the head (latency). These two factors will, of course, be related to the rotational speed of the disc and also the number of tracks. The following is an example of an exchangeable disc store.

Each disc unit carries one disc pack of six 14 in discs giving a total of ten recording surfaces. There are 200 recording tracks per surface, each divided into eight blocks. A block has the capacity to record 512 characters, giving 4 096 characters per track, 819 200 characters per surface and 8 192 000 characters per unit. Each character is held in six bits, four characters making the basic unit of storage—a 24-bit word. It is possible to link 8 units simultaneously on-line, giving a maximum on-line storage capacity of 65.536 million characters.

The discs revolve at 2400 rev/min, each surface having one moveable head. Transfer rate is 208 k ch/s and average access time 97.5 ms made up of average latency 12.5 ms and average seek time 85 ms. Cylinder capacity is 40 960 characters.

2. Mode of recording

As in the case of other forms of magnetic storage media, the basic recording unit is a binary digit (a bit) recorded magnetically on the disc surface. In contrast to magnetic tape, where a pattern of bits is recorded across the tape surface representing a character, bits on a disc are recorded serially along a track. This raises one obvious problem not encountered in tape recording, that of distinguishing the beginning and end of each character group of bits. The most commonly used, although not the only method of accomplishing this is to sub-divide each track sector, or block as it is usually known into standard sized groups of bits, usually six, each group capable of holding one character.

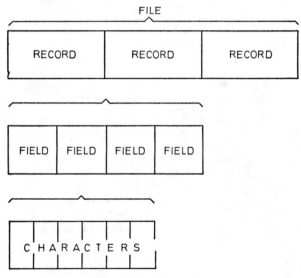

Figure 7.8. File organisation

Read/write operations essentially are in response to instructions to transfer data to and from central store. Such an instruction involves initially addressing the location on disc to be accessed, and the mechanical and switching operations already described. Data to be written to disc is assembled in store and the write instruction will quote both its location in store and the location of the designated storage area on disc. Similarly, a read instruction will also quote the location on disc and the store location into which data is to be accepted. A check on the write operations is incorporated into most systems. Having recorded data on one revolution of the disc it is read back during the next revolution for comparison with the original reading in store.

3. Organisation of data

Let us remind ourselves that the data we wish to store is in the form of files, for example, stock control file, sales ledger file, or wages file. The file is made up of a number of records, i.e. data relating to each stock item, each customer and each employee. In turn each record will consist of a number of data fields and each field a number of characters.

The storage medium we are using consists of a number of disc surfaces, each containing a number of recording tracks and in turn sub-divided into sectors. Each sector is able to record a standard number of bits marshalled into small groups, each group holding one character. If then a file, of the format we have described above is to be held on a device with these physical properties, then a number of considerations are relevant:

(a) *Location of records.* An essential feature in storing records on any type of file is that it must be possible to gain access to them when required. We have seen, in magnetic tape file systems, that access can only be gained sequentially for all practical purposes, but the essence of a disc file system is that records should be directly accessible. Each track sector on the disc surface is uniquely addressable in terms of surface, track and sector numbers. In turn each record is identifiable by a unique record key. The association of these two references in an indexing system will provide a means of locating records. A number of techniques are used in devising different types of indexing systems and these will be discussed in a later chapter.

(b) *Accommodating records.* In as much as we are dealing with a fixed unit of storage space, for example, a sector or block as it is often known with a recording capacity of 512 characters, it would be unrealistic to expect a situation in which all data records fit neatly into a single block. Systems considerations will determine the number of blocks that will conveniently hold a data record, and the name given to this unit of systems defined storage is a *bucket.* However, in a file using variable length records, the situation will arise when a record becomes too long to be accommodated in a single bucket. It would obviously be impractical to continue the record into the adjacent bucket as this will probably already contain another data record. Although as we shall see later the mode of file organisation will have a bearing on the problem, in principle the record will be accommodated on another part of the disc where there is room for it and a reference inserted in its original location giving the address of its new home. In effect the message says 'The record you are looking for is no longer here, it has been moved to such and such an address.'

This inserted redirecting reference is usually known as *tag*, although sometimes it is referred to as a *pointer*. The track in which the record was originally located, or should have been located, is known as the *home* track, while that to which it has been moved is known as the *overflow track* (Figure 7.9).

(c) *Allocating storage locations.* The very large storage capacity of a disc pack means that a number of different record files could well be found on the same set of discs. Bearing in mind that the greatest time element in tracing a specific record within a file is in moving the read/write head to locate the relevant track (*seek time*), this time factor can be reduced by organising data records within a file in a way that will minimise head movements.

Since the heads are fixed in relation to one another so that all are positioned over the same track on each surface simultaneously the whole of the data recorded on these 10 tracks can be read without further movement of the head. This leads to the concept of allocating storage space to files in a vertical plane, that is on tracks positioned vertically above one another on all discs, rather than on a horizontal plane, that is, a whole disc surface. The name given to a set of tracks used in this way (see Figure 7.10) is a *cylinder*. Of course a number of adjacent cylinders may be required to accommodate any one data file, but the technique gives a seek area that maximises the amount of data that can be accessed without further mechanical movement of the read/write heads.

(d) *Sequence of records.* Consideration needs to be given to the order in which records making up a file are stored. Whether they are stored in a definite order or indeed no order at all is a systems consideration which we will consider in more detail when discussing file structure.

READ/WRITE OPERATIONS

As with any other peripheral device, read/write operations are the subject of program instruction. Data to be written is assembled in an output section of store and the instruction will define both the core

86

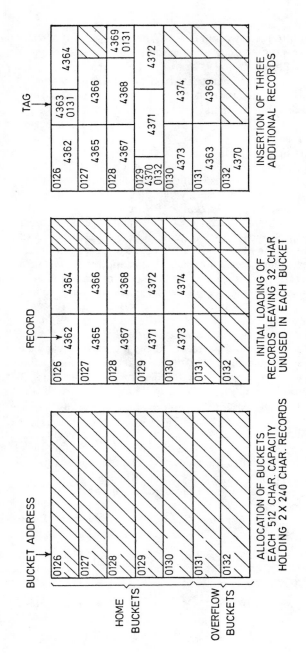

Figure 7.9. Storage of records on disc

address of the data and the designated location on the disc pack. In the same way a read instruction will quote the location on disc holding the data and also the input core locations to receive it. Since record identification and storage address are indexed, a read/write operation will be preceded by an operation to locate the address of the record.

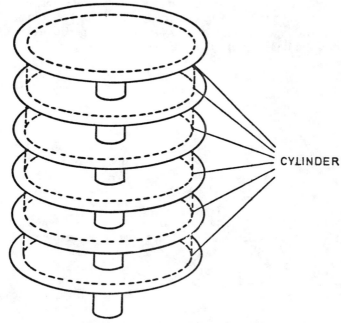

CYLINDER

Figure 7.10. Schematic storage cylinder

In most systems the unit of transfer to and from the processor is a bucket, and usually a check cycle is incorporated. Data is written during one revolution of the disc and in the next revolution read back to ensure an accurate transfer.

OPERATION SPEEDS AND CAPACITY

These vary a great deal from manufacturer to manufacturer and from model to model, and are therefore a little meaningless unless associated with a particular model. The range of capacity in characters is very wide both in fixed and exchangeable disc systems, and will, of course, depend on the number and size of discs on any one transport. For fixed discs from a system using 2 disc surfaces with a capacity of 2 million characters to one using 50 surfaces with over 400 million

characters, while exchangeable discs will vary from 10 surfaces holding
4 million characters to 20 surfaces holding well over 200 million.

By the same token, data transfer rates will vary between about
150 K and 300 K. As we have already seen, access time on a fixed disc
system will depend to a great extent on the number of read/write heads
per surface. It may be as low as 2 ms or as high as 100 ms. In an exchangeable disc system using one head per surface access time falls
generally within the 40 ms to 100 ms range. A specific example of
capacities and timings is given on page 83.

SYSTEMS CONSIDERATIONS

Perhaps systems considerations could be best reviewed by the
following comparison with tape storage systems.

	Tape	*Disc*
ACCESS	Only serial. In any given position only the next and (reverse reading) the last block can be read.	Non-serial. Any record on disc can be read next, although access time will depend on how records organised.
SECURITY	Blocks cannot be in-serted in middle of tape without making subsequent blocks illegible. Makes tape families, Grandfather, Father, Son necessary giving security against accidental corruption.	Blocks can be inserted but, although secured by prog-ram checks which allow only right program to access file, risk of over-write corruption probably greater than tape. Files can periodically be dumped on tape to provide re-construct to safeguard against corruption.
COST	Reel of tape costs around £20 and holds say 15-25 million characters. For efficient use four tape transports necessary. Controller and transport costs say 25 % less than disc. From cost point of view suitable for large files infrequently up-dated.	Disc pack costs around £300 and holds say 8 million characters. Can be efficient and useful one at a time. Controller and transport costs greater than tape. Applications where files are small and where non-serial access is important.

OTHER
CONSIDERATIONS

Of course, some processing modes will preclude choice between serial and non-serial recording devices. Real-time systems, time sharing systems requiring random access to records, and systems interrogation, none of these can be operated on tape backing storage.

While the two most popular forms of backing store generally in use are magnetic tape and disc, three other types must be mentioned briefly. These are magnetic drums and cards, and strips, and, for the small visible record computer, magnetic stripes.

MAGNETIC DRUMS

This device consists essentially of a cylinder coated with magnetisable material. The surface is divided into a number of tracks, each track in turn divided into a number of recording segments each uniquely addressable through the track and sector reference. The drum is permanently mounted in the device where it rotates at high speed.

In the early days of computers they were used as a central processor immediate access store either on their own or to back up a small core store. With the advent of ferrite cores they have, over the past few years, tended to fall into disuse, although more recently they have been reintroduced as a form of high speed access backing store.

Reading and writing to drums is through the medium of heads aero-dynamically floated over the drum surface. In most drum systems a one head per track principle is used although some systems on the market have a number of moveable heads each accessing a small number of adjacent tracks. The high speed access that one head per track systems provides is due to the elimination of seek time, that is, head movement. Access time is limited to the time taken for the drum to rotate bringing the required record under the read/write head. A way of minimising this rotational delay time and so provide very fast access is to speed up the rotation of the drum and to reduce its diameter. Among the fastest of drum systems, a 10½ in diameter drum rotating at over 7 000 m.p.m. will give an average access time of 4.25 ms, and data transfer rates of nearly 1 500 K characters per second.

The storage capacity of drums varies widely for different designs of device from say 1.5 million to 130 million characters. As a general rule, however, the greater the capacity, the longer of access time (Figure 7.11). A number of drum units can be fitted on-line to the central processor, giving a massive backing storage facility. Due to the fast access time offered by some drum systems, compared with discs, these lend themselves to use in time-sharing systems and interrogating

procedures where fast access times and data transfer rates are called
for in the process of repeatedly loading different programs and locating
and retrieving data.

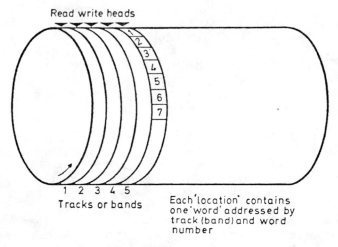

Figure 7.11. Magnetic drum

MAGNETIC CARDS

The main difference in principle between magnetic cards and other
forms of magnetic storage is that the recording surface is physically
broken down to a number of individual fairly small areas of about
50 to 70 in^2 although card sizes vary from system to system, for
example, 16 in × 4½ in or 14 in × 3½ in. Cards are made of a plastic
such as *Mylar* and have a recording surface divided into a number of
parallel tracks, each track recording a number of characters. Records
are addressable through card and track references. Capacities will
depend on card size, number of tracks and packing density, but, depending on the system, a single card surface will hold between 165 K
and 216 K characters.

Cards are assembled in cartridges and, when a cartridge is fitted
into the device, individual cards are selected by means of a unique
pattern of notches along the top edge of the card. When a card is selected
it drops from the cartridge, is transported mechanically through a race
and passes over a 7 in diameter capstan where it is held on the capstan
surface by vacuum. Suspended above the capstan are read/write heads
and the card passes through the narrow gap between them (Figure 7.12).

It is usual to mount a number of moveable read/write heads opposite the capstan capable of moving over a number of tracks. For example, 36 heads moving to any one of four positions so covering operations on 144 tracks. The total storage capacity of a magnetic card device can be very high. With, say 256 cards in a cartridge, and the device capable of holding a magazine of eight cartridges a storage capacity of over 5000 million characters is given.

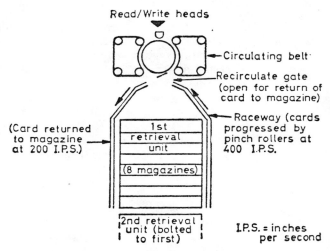

Figure 7.12. Schematic card storage

Due to the rather involved mechanical processes, movement of card to capstan and positioning of reading head, access times are slow, varying between approximately 200 ms and 500 ms. The mechanics of the device can also present a problem, some users having expressed doubts as to the security of the recording medium. With cards travelling through the device at a maximum rate of 380 inches a second there is a possibility of damage when a card is retrieved. Reconstruction of the information it contains could then become a difficult and time consuming process.

MAGNETIC STRIPS

The IBM Datacell system uses as a recording medium magnetisable strips about 2¼ × 13 in divided in 100 recording tracks each of 2 000 bytes capacity. Strips are assembled in groups of 10 forming a sub-cell, and an assembly of 20 sub-cells form a cell. In shape a cell is rather like a segment of a cylinder. A magazine in cylindrical form will contain up to 10 cells giving a total drive capacity of 2 000 strips. Cells are self-contained units of storage and can be fitted to or withdrawn from the magazine as required.

For read/write operation, individual strips are selected by reference to a coding tab for identification, and extracted from the cell as the circular magazine rotates beneath a capstan. The strip is wrapped around the capstan passing under 20 read/write heads positioned near it, the capstan rotates at 1 200 rev/min, thus forming, in effect, a small magnetic drum. These heads are moveable into five different positions, giving access to the 100 strip tracks. When the read/write operation is complete the strip is returned to its sub-cell by reversing the direction of the capstan movement. When organising the storage of data on this device the 'cylinder' concept is used, related data items being recorded on each successive fifth track thus eliminating the need for head movement. In this way each strip will contain five cylinders each of 20 tracks.

Total capacity of a full magazine, or array, containing 10 data cells is 400 million bytes, while maximum access time is 600 ms.

MAGNETIC STRIPES

This is the form of storage generally used in small Visible Record Computers and will be discussed in detail in a later chapter.

EXERCISES

1. Distinguish between 'immediate access storage' and 'backing storage' giving four examples of the latter.

2. Give a short description of how data is organised in a magnetic tape file.

3. What is the purpose of (a) a header label, and (b) a trailer label? Give some indication of the contents of these two labels.

4. Give a brief discription of an application for which you feel magnetic tape would be the best form of backing storage.

5. Describe how data is organised on an exchangeable disc backing store.

6. Two of the ways of processing records are known as serial and sequential processing. Show how these two modes differ.

7. Give a short description of how data is recorded on a magnetic disc store.

8. What do you understand by the terms 'seek-time' and 'rotational delay' in connection with disc storage?

9. Describe how a computer deals with the situation whem more records are designated for storage in a location on disc than the location is capable of holding.

10. What safeguards are incorporated into the hardware of a computer to prevent mis-writing or mis-reading information in the case of magnetic disc storage?

8

Organisation of Data

It has been said that data is the raw material of a data processing system, and that the system itself involves a series of procedures designed to relate and interpret data items in order to produce meaningful information in a pre-determined form. When we come to examine data in a little detail, we find that data items fall within a number of different but fairly well defined categories. If we use a simple illustration from a sales ledger system, information for each customer will be on record as follows:

23456	F. G. Brown, 12 High Street,	£146.00
(Account	Oxbridge	(Balance
Number)	(Customer Name and address)	outstanding)

We can divide this record into two main elements.

Firstly, that part which identifies the customer which is purely descriptive by nature. This is data which we would not expect to change very frequently; in fact, unless the customer changes his name and address, it will always remain the same. This quality gives rise to data of this type being referred to as *static*. However, part of this descriptive data is not strictly speaking necessary to the identification of the customer, that is, the account number. This is really an accountancy convenience to enable us to readily find an account when required and to provide a logical sequence in which accounts can be filed. For this reason, it is frequently known as *control* data.

The second element in this record is the quantitative part—the balance—which we would expect to change quite frequently as more goods are sold or as payment is made. This is known as *dynamic* data since it is constantly being up-dated to provide a statement of the current situation.

We have then three different types of data item, control, static and dynamic, all of which can be present in one data record. In the same way, data records themselves fall within a number of defined categories. Looked at from the simplest level and again using a sales ledger system to illustrate the point, in a manual system three basic types of record can be identified:

(a) Data recording in detail individual transactions with the customer, i.e. invoices, records of payment, credit notes.

(b) Data summarising the records in (a) and providing an up to date statement of the position of each customer. These are the ledger accounts.

(c) Information derived from (a) and (b) used for control and statistical purposes, sales analysis, control accounts, debtor lists etc.

These three types of record are known as *input, master* and *output* records respectively. Having established the principle of defined types of data and of records, let us now turn our attention to computer processing and review the structure these elements take in computer storage.

COMPUTER FILES

In any system whether it is manually, mechanically or electronically processed, information is held on files. Each file being a collection of data records related to a specific aspect of the system of which it is part.

While a record will relate to one specific unit in a system, i.e. one account, or one item of stock, it may nevertheless contain more than one data statement relating to that unit. For example, in a sales ledger

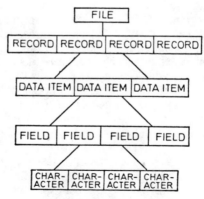

Fig. 8.1. File data levels

system, a record could contain just the customer identification and the balance outstanding on a given date. On the other hand, the record could start with a statement of balance followed by a series of transaction items, sales, credits, and payments, all relating to that one account. Thus a record may be made up of a series of data items, each consisting of a number of data fields, each field a number of characters and each character expressed, for computer storage purposes, in binary digits. A computer file can, therefore, be broken down into a number of levels (Figure 8.1).

Now, if in a practical situation, all of these elements were of the same length, then their organisation in storage would be a fairly straight-forward business and a very high level of efficiency would be attained in the use of storage space. We know, however, from experience, that this does not happen. The number of characters in names and addresses varies considerably and the number of digits in expressions of quantity are far from constant. It will be evident that, in recording on any magnetic media some definition must be made to segregate record from record, item from item, and so on, otherwise the recording will just be one continuous meaningless succession of characters.

One way of approaching this problem is to artificially standardise the record length, and the length of its sub-divisions by allocating a fixed amount of storage space for each. These are known as *fixed length records*. Of course, to do this, the fixed storage space would have to be sufficient to accommodate the longest record we anticipate, so any record shorter than the maximum would lead to unused and so wasted storage. Also, time would be wasted at the input and output stage as it would take just as long to 'read' those locations not con-taining relevant data as it would do if data was recorded in them. On the credit side, programming is easier as a fixed record length precludes the need to identify record lengths and the storage space required for specifying such lengths is saved.

To make optimum use of available storage space, a system that uses only just that space required for each record is called for. These are known as *variable length records*. However, the point made earlier that record lengths must be defined if stored information is to be meaningful means that the length of each individual record must be in some way signalled or recorded.

Now this can be done either by interposing a special pattern of bits to indicate the end of each element of data or by recording before each record a count of the number of characters, fields, etc., contained in each data element. Variable length record working has the advantage of economising in storage space, but programming and software routines become more complicated.

However, fixed length records and variable length records represent two extremes; between these extremes there is room for utilising both the fixed and the variable length principles. The record design in a system may allow for a fixed number of items of variable length or, on the other hand, a variable number of items of fixed length.

Within a data record, then, data items can be specified in the following modes:

> Variable number of items of *variable* length
> Fixed number of items of *variable* length
> Variable number of items of *fixed* length
> Fixed number of items of *fixed* length

The same considerations apply to the data fields that make up each data item where again storage space may be allocated on a basis of either a fixed or a variable number of characters to each field, and a fixed or variable number of fields to a data item. It should be emphasised however, that within a given data file only one of these alternatives can be present. It is impractical for example to have some data items modelled on a variable-variable principle and others on a variable-fixed principle.

CLASSIFICATION OF COMPUTER FILES

As we saw earlier, input, master and output records will be present in a processing system when looked at from the simplest level. An assembly of each of these types of record is a computer file. As a general rule, the files present in a data processing system are:

(a) *Input files* contain records of the day by day events and transactions related to the system of which the file is part. In the case of a sales ledger system, these would include details of goods despatched to customers, payments received, goods returned and discounts allowed. These are known as movement records. Records related to the addition, deletion and change of status of customers on file, usually referred to as changes, are assembled on a separate input file.

(b) *Master files.* These represent the core of the system and represent the storage of the total information relating to the system. Two distinct types of file could well be present:

(i) Those containing standard information to which reference has to be made frequently. For example, the equivalent of a price list from which can be read the unit prices of goods despatched to customers and thus provide the basis for the preparation of invoices.

(ii) Those files containing all the data relating to each element contained in the file. For example, in a sales ledger system this could well be the equivalent of a ledger card containing customer identification and status information, opening balance, movement, debit and credit items and closing balance.

(c) *Output files.* These carry the information to produce the end product called for by the systems programs. Usually information extracted from or computed from the master files, such as end of month sales statement for printing and distribution to customers, or a list of current account balances for control purposes.

(d) *Transfer files.* These are intermediary files that may be necessary to hold information when a number of stages are involved in the processing cycle.

(e) *Program files,* holding the application program and also standard sub-routines that may be called for during processing.

Having reviewed the types of file that may be present in a computer processing system, let us remind ourselves of the basic routine involved in the interaction of backing storage and the central processor store.

If it were practical to store the total volume of all the files and records associated with a given system in the immediate access store, then an ideal situation would result where every item of data would be immediately available for processing. However, such a store would need to accommodate the millions of characters making up the files and would be prohibitively expensive. As a second best, then, we give the central processor access to the mass of information held on backing store by requiring it to transfer between itself and these stores small blocks of records, as and when it requires, and of a size it can readily accommodate.

Now, of course, two basic pre-requisites must be present for this transfer to take place meaningfully. Each record must be (a) *identifiable* and (b) *locateable.*

IDENTIFYING RECORDS

In order to distinguish the one particular record required for processing it must contain some unique factor. This factor is known as the *record key.* By this we mean that the key must be unique in a given file. Of course, a record in an input file may hold the same key as one in a master file if the system calls for the former to be applied to the latter in a process of up-dating. Now the usual way of providing such a key, is to allocate to each record a group of characters and or digits, known as a code. It is a system with which we are all familiar in the form of bank account numbers and social security numbers. In fact we find that in most aspects of our life which involves a clear identification, a number, or code, is used.

CODING DESIGN

Such a unique reference to records provided for any data processing system can also accomplish a number of useful factors, particularly in the area of computer processing where records cannot be identified, or examined by visual scrutiny. The code will give us:

(a) The means of identifying a record without reference to the descriptive data contained in the record.
(b) A medium for sorting records into a pre-determined order, or into defined groups based on some record characteristic, for example, geographical zones, or product groups.
(c) An easy way of matching records that relate to each other such as bringing movement and master records together.
(d) Economies can be effected in data recording. The use of a code can eliminate the need to repeat descriptive data. For example, there is no need to record a part specification on a stock control movement record since this can be copied, if required, from the master file record.
(e) It makes possible record indexing by associating the record key with a physical store location address.
(f) It can specify the processing routine. For example, the last digit could indicate whether cash or credit sales and so indicate the routine to be followed.
(g) A code may specify physical characteristics by relating elements of the code to factors such as size or volume.
(h) It can show relationships with other items, by for example, one element of the code being common to all parts of a sub-assembly, while the remaining elements defining each individual part of the assembly.

In fact, broadly speaking, a code can be made to do anything. It is simply giving a label or a series of labels to indicate a quality or a series of qualities about a commodity or a record of activity. Of course, the more we expect from a code, the more complex will be its construction and the more unwieldly its size.

TYPES OF CODE

Codes used in data processing systems fall into two categories:

1. Non-significant.
2. Significant.

Non-significant codes, as the name suggests, do not attempt in any way to describe the factor to which they relate. In themselves, they are meaningless and the range of purposes they serve very limited. Such a code may be used to identify a record, as a medium for sorting records into code number sequence and for record matching purposes but little else. They are simple to construct, for example, all that is needed is a block of numbers, say 0001-9999. They involve the use of a minimum number of digits in their construction and make use of all the combinations in the sequence without leaving gaps. These are sometimes referred to as sequential or serial codes.

The construction of a significant code will be based on those factors within a record that require to be identified. The combinations of such codes are infinite, but one or more of the following basic principles could well be incorporated.

Block codes

These are used to identify groups or blocks of records having a common property. The group is usually indicated by the first digit in the code and the remaining digits allocated serially to those records falling within the group. A simple geographical coding of sales ledger accounts could be:

Account Number	
	10000 – 19999 S.W. Area.
	20000 – 29999 S.E. Area.
	30000 – 39999 Home Counties.

Such a coding principle allows for a more detailed grouping and the second digit might be used to signify a sub-group with the main grouping.

Account Number	
	10000 – 10999 S. W. Area–Cornwall.
	11000 – 11999 S.W. Area – Devon.
	12000 – 12999 S.W. Area – Somerset.

It will be evident that the greater the degree of analysis required from the coding system, the greater the number of digits required to form the code. The range of number combinations used serially to allocate individual records within a sub-group, must be large enough to accommodate the largest group. Since the number of records in each sub-group is likely to vary considerably a large proportion of the codes will remain unused.

This block coding principle is used extensively in data processing systems having the advantages of simple construction and adaptability. It is comparatively easy to delete and insert groups, and the system lends itself readily to visual checks and provides a medium for sorting into the defined areas and districts and for retrieving information relevant to a particular area or district.

Significant digit codes

These are codes that incorporate a quantitative element in the form of an actual measurement of an attribute of a commodity. For example, the coding the copper piping could be:

264013 — 13 mm diameter
264022 — 22 mm diameter
264027 — 27 mm diameter

The significant digits of the code, in this case, those defining diameter, are usually part of a longer code which may incorporate a second coding principle, and in this the first digit 2 could represent plumbing fittings, the second 6 copper fittings, the third pipe and the last two the diameter of the pipe. While this type of code has the advantage that it accurately describes a commodity in detail and so is very useful in a visual context there are drawbacks in its use in computer data processing systems. It is not always possible to define a measurement in numeric terms which may result in a mixed alpha/numeric element in the code as could well be the case with paper sizes, A4, A5 and so on.

Hierarchial codes

These are 'tree' type codes using a series of levels of sub-divisions. Its most important feature is to indicate the inter-relationship of the

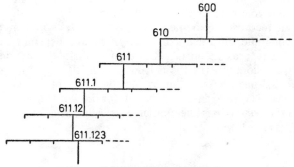

Figure 8.2. Tree-hierarchical codes

600   Useful arts. Applied science.
610   Medicine.
611   Medicine—Anatomy.
611.1   Medicine—Anatomy—Circulatory system.
611.12   Medicine—Anatomy—Circulatory system—Heart.
611.123   Medicine—Anatomy—Circulatory system—Heart—Left.

coded items. The most widely used example of this type of code is the
Dewey universal decimal code used for indexing library books (Figure
8.2).

RECORD KEY
   The purpose of all the coding systems mentioned so far, is to enable
the construction of a record key that will identify a specific record.
Associating this key with a location address through an indexing
process, enables the retrieval of any required record. In fact we can go
further than this, the key can be constructed in such a way that, by
giving components of the record a common element in the key, all
records falling within a specified category can be retrieved by reference
to the key.
   For example on file a record is held:

   46792   B. Smith, 149 High Street, Newtown, Sussex.

If the key 46792 is non-significant (i.e. purely arbitrarily allocated
without reference to the subject content of the record) then its use is
limited to the retrieval of that one record and that alone. This is usually
known as key retrieval.
   If on the other hand the key incorporated a degree of significance,
for instance the digits 67 for any customer living in Sussex, then we
have at our disposal a means of retrieving records for all customers
living in that county. However it must be borne in mind that a search
through all records may be necessary to pick out those containing 67
as the second and third digits of the key. This will depend on the order
in which the records are organised. If the first digit '4' is common to all
sales ledger records, if the file is held sequential only that part of the
sequence '67' need be referred to. Another way of retrieving all the
'Sussex' records is to examine all records for the word 'Sussex'. This type
of record retrieval, that is selecting all records that meet specified criteria,
is known as *census retrieval.*

DESCRIPTORS
   In using this latter method to retrieve the required group of records,
that is a search for the description 'Sussex' we are using a factor divorced
from the construction of the record key and indeed independent of its
existence. A data field within the record is used for identification; this
is known as a *descriptor.*
   In the above example, it was easy enough to incorporate in the key
a geographical identification. It could well be the case, however, that a
record contains such a range of characteristics that it would be im-

practical to construct a key containing them all. Under these circumstances, if we require an information retrieval routine that will locate the record on quoting any of these characteristics, then the use of descriptors is the only practical way of doing this.

While it is beyond the scope of this book to discuss in detail the use and the indexing of descriptors, the following basic points can be made.

(a) A key-word in each data item is selected to indicate its characteristic. This is known as a descriptor.

(b) A record may contain a number of descriptors, one for each characteristic.

(c) Information retrieval in its simplest form would involve searching all records sequentially and testing for the combination of descriptors in order to locate those containing the characteristics looked for.

(d) To overcome the problem of a search through all records, indexes can be constructed associating the descriptor with the location in which records are held, or with the record key.

To go back to our original example, if this was expanded as follows we have a very simple example of associating descriptors with keys through a process of what is known as *co-ordinate* indexing:

46792   B. Smith, 149 High Street, Newtown, Sussex.
Discount on Sales 15 %
Outlet for product red

Then taking as descriptors 'Sussex', '15 %' and 'Red' we could build up an index

	Location of key numbers				
Sussex	149,	176,	284,	867,	942
15 %	165,	284,	389,	672,	867
Red	102,	165,	243,	284,	732

Retrieval of details of all customers living in Sussex would be by reference to all keys referenced against Sussex.

Customers living in Sussex granted 15 % discount would be contained in those records indexed against both Sussex and 15 %, while customers purchasing product Red in Sussex at 15 % discount would involve a coincidence of keys against the three descriptors.

EXERCISES

1. What is the difference between (a) master data, (b) movement data? Give examples of these two types of data from a system with which you are familiar.

2. Data records may be of fixed or variable length. Distinguish between these and describe how a computer will distinguish between the beginning of one and the end of another record in both cases.

3. Give a short description of the types of file that are used in a commercial data processing system.

4. What do you understand by a record key? What purpose does this serve when incorporated as part of a file record?

5. Explain the difference between a significant and a non-significant code. Give an example of the use of the former.

6. A data field within a record may be selected for use a descriptor. Explain the purpose of this illustrating your answer with an example.

7. Give an account of the main types of coding that can be used in a data processing system.

8. Explain what is meant by the following terms in relation to data files held on magnetic tape:
       (a) File maintenance
       (b) File label
       (c) File protection.

9

Programming and Software

We have seen earlier that an essential element in any data processing system is the set of instructions that determine processing functions and control the operation of the whole processing routine. The collective term by which these sets of instructions are known is *software*.

In computer data processing, three main categories of software can be identified, they are:

Programming software.
Operating software.
Utility software.

As with data records, it will be appreciated that the instructions comprising software routines need to be stored on one medium or another, and sets of instructions ultimately read into the processor's store to be available for immediate access and execution. Broadly speaking the same techniques are used for software storage as for data. Initially instructions are recorded in punched card or punched paper tape form, and indeed, in some cases, these represent their permanent storage media, and are read into store through card or tape readers every time the routine has to be processed. There are, however, major disadvantages to this form of software storage, a fair amount of off-line storage space is required, setting up and reading in card and paper tape files is a comparatively lengthy process and the risk of damage and, in the case of a card file, loss of records, is relatively high.

Whilst, for initial input, software will probably be prepared in card or paper tape form, the disadvantages associated with this will, to a large extent be overcome by writing to and storing permanently on a magnetic storage medium such as magnetic tape or disc. However, while set-up and read in time will be faster, storage more convenient and the risk of damage and loss reduced, closer attention will need to be paid to problems associated with ensuring that the correct routine is identified and loaded.

Storage on discs linked on-line to the system means that software can be readily accessed as and when required although their capacity and the number of transports available will present a limiting factor. The cost of storage in this form will, of course, be very much higher than magnetic tapes.

PROGRAMMING SOFTWARE

Sometimes known as systems programs, a program represents the assembling together in sequence of all of those instructions necessary to carry out a pre-determined task, specifying all those procedures to be applied to data entering the system. The program will call in data records as and when they are required for processing, organise their allocation to store locations and their movement in store, test the data with pre-determined criteria to decide which processing functions should be applied, specify arithmetic and logical operations and marshall the results for output in the form required.

The format of the program instruction strictly conforms to a set of rules which in themselves define a program language. Many different programming languages have been developed at varying levels of sophistication, some to meet the needs of specific makes of hardware while others, of more universal nature, orientated towards specialised processing requirements.

Machine codes

From the machine point of view, to enable processing to take place, two basic items of information must be communicated. These are, one, a specification of the action to be taken and two, an identification of the data on which this action is to be performed. This gives us the basic structure of a program instruction, the former known as the *operation* and the latter the *operand*.

Furthermore, the machine can only act on instructions communicated to it in a format it has been designed to recognise; thus a defined pattern of binary bits will cause the machine to perform a defined operation. A set of these numeric codes designed to cover the whole range of machine operations is known as a *computer instruction code* or a *machine code*. Again, the machine can only identify the item of data on which an operation is to be performed by virtue of its position or location in store.

Since each location carries a unique reference or address, again from the machine viewpoint a binary code representing the address is called for. Of course, a programmer writing out instructions using machine codes and store locations would use decimal digits instead of binary statements. These digits, on being punched into card or tape and fed through a reader, would automatically be converted into the equivalent binary string capable of being stored and acted upon by the computer. The construction of a program in this form is known as a *machine code language.*

Assembly languages

The next development in programming was, in order to simplify writing procedures, to substitute a mneumonic, for example, ADD instead of say 38, the machine code, in the operation part of the instruction, and a description of the data, for example, Sales instead of 1456, the address location, in the operand part. The word 'Sales' is known as the symbolic address in contrast to 1456, the absolute address.

Of course, an instruction in mneumonic form such as ADD, SUB, MLT or DIV could well mean that a series of individual machine instructions need to be executed in order to carry it out, and it is therefore, usually referred to as a MACRO instruction.

A computer language making use of these principles, mneumonics to define operations and symbolic addresses is known as an *assembly language.*

We established above that the computer is only able to recognise and take action on instructions communicated to it in terms of machine codes and absolute addresses. It is therefore necessary to convert, or translate, the assembly language to this basic form. This is done through

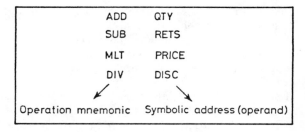

Figure 9.1. Example of assembly code statements

the medium of a special program known as an *assembler* which in effect associates each assembly language statement with its equivalent machine code instructions and so converts the assembly language into a form acceptable to the computer. The program before conversion is known as a source program and, when assembled, into machine instructions as an object program. An example of an assembly language is given in Figure 9.1.

'High-level' languages

The use of machine codes and assembly languages have the disadvantage that a problem needs to be broken down and stated in terms and in a format corresponding to the machine instruction format, that is, *operation* and *operand*. For this reason, they are known as machine orientated or computer orientated languages.

From a programmer's point of view, the process would be much simplified if instructions could be structured to follow much the same pattern as a written or verbal statement of the problem. To accomplish this, an extension of the principle of Macro instructions was called for, each instruction generating a number of sets of machine code instructions in contrast to an assembly statement generating one set. These more complex Macro instructions are known as auto-code statements and a computer language making use of them known as 'problem orientated'. Examples of these statements are shown in Figure 9.2.

Of course, the same consideration applies to these 'high level' languages as to assembly 'low level' languages, that is the need to convert auto-code statements into the acceptable machine code. This is accomplished by the use of a more sophisticated conversion program, known as a *compiler* program.

Standard languages

Two problems arise in the development of problem orientated computer languages constructed on the auto-code principle. The first is the tendency of manufacturers to develop languages that are designed for use on their own machines and secondly, the difficulties involved in constructing a language to cope with all processing needs, mathematical, scientific and commercial.

Co-operation between manufacturers and users led to the development of standard languages, the use of which was not dependent on any particular make of machine. Initially, separate languages were constructed to cover the two main processing areas, business systems and mathematical problems, and indeed these are in widespread use today. One language COBOL (Common Business Orientated Language) for use in the business systems sector and two languages ALGOL (Algorithmic Language) and FORTRAN (Formula Translation) for applications in the mathematical sector, the first of these being a European development and the second its American equivalent. A later development resulted in the production of one universal language capable of dealing with both commercial and mathematical applications. This, first published in 1966, is known as PL/1.

```
SEQUENCE No.
1 2 3 4 5 6 | 7 | 8 9 10 11 | 12 ... 60
001010  IDENTIFICATION DIVISION.
001020  PROGRAM-ID. STOCK-VAL.
           ---ETC---
001200  ENVIRONMENT DIVISION.
001210  CONFIGURATION SECTION.
001220  SOURCE-COMPUTER. DECSYSTEM-10.
001230  OBJECT-COMPUTER. DECSYSTEM-10.
           ---ETC---
001410  PROCEDURE DIVISION.
001420  PARA-1.
001430      OPEN INPUT CARD-FILE.
001440      OPEN OUTPUT PRINT-FILE.
001450      MOVE SPACES TO P-REC.
           ---ETC---
001510  PARA-2.
001520      READ CARD FILE AT END GO TO PARA-5.
001530      MOVE S-CODE TO P-CODE.
           ---ETC---
001600  PARA-3.
001610      MULTIPLY RPRICE BY QUANTITY GIVING SVALUE.
001620      ADD SVALUE TO TVALUE.
001630      MOVE SVALUE TO P-VALUE.
           ---ETC---
```

Figure 9.2. Problem orientated statements in COBOL

While, as mentioned above, the thinking behind these developments was to produce machine independent languages, the problem of differing machine specifications remained. This was overcome by manufacturers

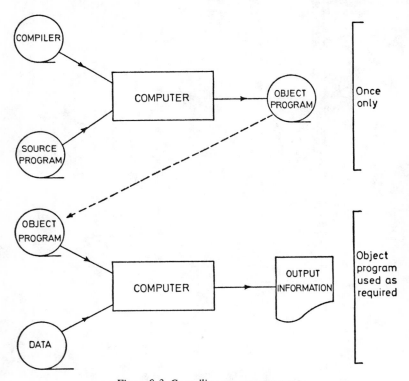

Figure 9.3. Compiling a source program

producing their own compilers capable of accepting these common language statements and converting them into the particular machine instruction format acceptable to their own machines.

With the advent of interrogating procedures through remote terminals, the need was established for relatively simple languages that could be used through manual operation of a keyboard. The most generally accepted such language is known as BASIC. It provides a powerful tool for using a computer in a conversational mode. Figure 9.4 shows specimen program statements in BASIC.

In spite of the above developments in common languages there remains a problem of adapting programs, not written in a standard language, for use on other machines. For this purpose specialised programs can be obtained from manufacturers known as *simulators*. These permit the conversion of a program written in a machine dependent language to an object program acceptable to another make of machine. Alternatively, the simulator may be stored in the computer enabling the old program to be executed.

```
10  LET A = 0
20  LET B = 0
30  FOR I = 1 TO 75
40  READ M
50  IF M >100 THEN 140
60  LET A = A + M
65  PRINT A
70  IF M >39 THEN 90
80  LET B = B + 1
90  NEXT I
100 LET C = A /4
110 PRINT "NUMBER OF FAILURES", B
120 PRINT "AVERAGE MARK", C
130 GOTO 160
140 PRINT "INVALID MARK", M
145 GOTO 90
150 DATA <75 NUMBERS >
160 END
```

Figure 9.4. Program statements in BASIC

APPLICATION PACKAGE PROGRAMS

In commercial data processing systems a number of elements are found that are common to the needs of many users operating the system. This is very evident in, for example, stock control, sales ledger, purchase ledger and wages systems. To avoid the need for programs to be separately written by or for each individual user, manufacturers offer standard application packages for a range of applications. The packages consist of the programs and sub-routines covering the processing requirements of a given system or procedure and will include input and output formats, and file specifications. The package can be varied within limits to suit a particular user's requirements.

Obviously, the acceptability of a package program will hinge on the extent of the changes that will have to be made to fit it in. These modifications would either be in the existing system or in the package itself. Should they be too extensive to be desirable or practical then a specially written program would be called for.

The advantages in the use of application packages are:

(a) They are economical.
(b) They are well documented, including a statement of objectives, detailed systems specification, identification of hardware requirement, input output and file specifications and systems timing.
(c) They are available at comparatively short notice.
(d) They are easy to use.

However, the critical question is—will it do the job required? If not, then the above advantages become meaningless. A further problem area in the use of packages is that they call for a minimum hardware configuration which may not, in the event, be available.

OPERATING SYSTEMS

An applications program is a series of instructions controlling the various procedures that are to be applied to data records. An operating system is a series of instructions that monitor and control the execution of these instructions, assigns and controls the use and activities of available hardware and indeed, under some circumstances, decides which program is to be operated at a given time. The operating system is stored in the central processor, but in contrast to the applications program, remains there permanently.

In the early days of computers, a great deal of manual intervention was necessary. Jobs were generally processed sequentially, the operator loading in the relevant program, supervising the reading in of data, possibly supervising processing activity through a console and at the end of the run unloading data files and output files, repeating this process for each job. In addition, the machine operated in this sequential way occupied itself first with reading in data, and on completing this would process the data and then output the results of processing.

An operating system eliminates the need for most of this operator intervention and also organises the use of the processing power of the computer in the most efficient way. However, it will be appreciated that if an operating system is going to control central processor and peripheral activity there must, of necessity, be provided the minimum hardware configuration consistent with the demands of the system.

It can be argued that, while manufacturers do not make a direct charge for operating systems, these are still expensive by virtue of the peripherals they demand and by the processor store space they occupy. For instance, 18 K of storage may well be permanently occupied by the system in a 48 K–256 K processor. However, these considerations

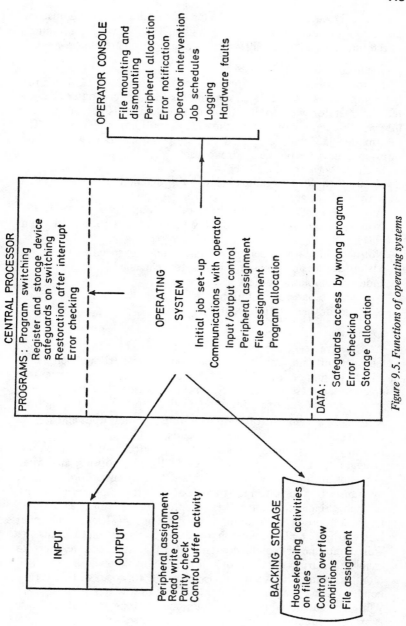

Figure 9.5. Functions of operating systems

are probably outweighed by the faster throughput and higher machine utilisation provided by an operating system. The following is a summary of the functions an operating system is designed to perform.

Communications with the operator

In the first generation of computers the operator had to instruct the computer. An operating system means that the computer can now tell the operator what to do, when his intervention is needed, and can inform the operator of actions the system itself has implemented. This information is usually conveyed to the operator through the medium of printed messages on the control console.

Such messages could include:

Request to load or unload data or program files to a specified peripheral device.

Automatic logging of machine time utilisation.

Notification of opening and closing of files with record count check.

Notification of assignment of peripheral units to specified files.

Listing of files and program required for scheduled jobs.

Indicate completion of job.

Notification of error conditions.

Request for operator intervention.

Hardware control

As we have seen, a computer configuration consists not only of a processing unit but also those input, output and storage peripherals necessary to support it. Efficient processing hinges on the harmonious interaction of these constituent parts. To provide this, the hardware control element of an operating system will perform the following:

Automatic assignment of peripheral units, input, output and storage as demanded by processing requirements.

In a multi-programming situation it will control switching from one program to another according to established priorities, and when programs are interrupted will safeguard the current records in store by transferring register and storage contents to temporary locations, re-establishing the position when the program recommences.

Perform house-keeping routines on files, checking header and trailer labels to agree record counts, purge dates, continuation files etc.

Will dump the complete contents of CPU store and registers to enable a restart in the event of a processing breakdown.

Monitor storage in direct access devices to cope with overflow conditions and guard against unintentional over-writes.

Will carry out initial machine set-up checks to assure that hardware is properly functioning and ready for processing runs.

Control and input and output

The operating system will control the flow of input data from backing storage to CPU as demanded by processing requirements. It will also organise the allocation of storage space to receive the data, will perform standard checks other than those validation procedures called for by the program such as parity checking and back spacing instructions in the event of a mis-read, and organise the transfer of input data held temporarily in buffer devices.

The system will organise the location of output data in store, supervise its transfer to an output peripheral, automatically assigning a peripheral device for this purpose, and will perform accuracy checks on the writing of data to the output medium.

Utility software

Utility programs are designed to carry out standard routines that are common to most applications. They are usually part of the manufacturer's software library and can be supplied to users as self-contained routines. Examples of procedures that form the subject of utility software are:

File Creation, maintenance and up-dating.
Sorting.
Merging.
Information retrieval routines.
Editing output records.
Copying files or records.

Again, as with the case of application packages the problem of compatability with a given system may arise, and in order to overcome this these programs are often written in the form of *generators*. This means that formats can be fixed by a programmer for a specific application, and the generator used in conjunction with the format definition to compile a program unique to the application.

LOW OR HIGH LEVEL LANGUAGES?

Having then seen that computer languages fall into these two main categories, the inevitable question arises. Which is best to use? In considering this we can ignore machine code language as nowadays for commercial systems applications this is never used. The manufacturer will write assembler and compiler programs to create machine code object programs.

We can compare low and high level languages under a number of different headings as follows:

Number of machine code instructions in object program?	Appreciably more for high level than low, in fact can be up to 50 % more for some routines.
Computer running time?	Since more instructions high level will take proportionally longer than low level.
IAS storage space?	Again more space needs to be allocated to high level program due to larger numbers of instructions.
Hardware?	High level languages demand a minimum core size (Accommodation of compiler) and minimum peripheral requirements that may not be essential with low level language. For example compiling a COBOL program will require at minimum three tape decks and 8 K of IAS and could be as high as 4 tape or two disc drives and 32 K of IAS.
Programming time?	Much less for high level language, could represent a saving of up to 40 % of programming time in low level.
Programmer training?	Training time to reach comparable levels of proficiency is around one-half for high level language compared with low.

The choice therefore, of high or low level languages is one of balance, assuming that minimum high level hardware requirements are available. Frequently run programs in low level language save probably more than the additional programming time and resultant expense in their preparation by economies in computer running time. For programs run fairly infrequently, probably the use of a high level language would be indicated. However, it must not be overlooked that one major advantage of high level languages is the capacity to use them on different makes of machines which might well be an overriding factor for large organisations using machines of more than one make.

ELEMENTS OF PROGRAM STRUCTURE

A program, in its basic machine code form, is a list of instructions compiled and assembled logically that will perform a specified operation or process. Each instruction in its simplest form contains an operation code defining what to do, and also an operand address identifying the data item on which the operation is to be carried out. Instructions are stored in sequence order in the processor's store, although they may not necessarily be stored in a completely consecutive range of addresses. Continuity of sequence must be preserved in the event of a gap in the range of addresses by a direction in the last of one sequence to the first in the next.

Having loaded the program, on the command Execute, the address in which the first instruction is located will be entered into a special register that controls the sequence in which instructions are followed, a sequence control register. The next step is to access the address specified in this register and copy the instruction it contains into an instruction register. There, the operation part of the instruction will be decoded and the relevant circuitry accessed to carry out the operation. In turn, access is made to the operand address to locate the data on which the operation is to be performed. The operation is then carried out, the next instruction in sequence transferred to the instruction register, and the cycle repeated.

While the above suggests that instructions are executed in strict sequence from the first to the last, this is not usually so as the procedure may call for alternative courses of action based on predetermined criteria. On the other hand, the procedure may call for some groups of instructions to be repeated.

Other than data movement instructions, i.e. the input and output of data, the following four basic routines will be evident in most programs. These are illustrated by the flow-chart (Figure 6.8).

(a) *Loops.* This occurs when a sequence of instructions are repeated for each item of data to which they refer, until the input of these data items is exhausted. If, for example, the routine called for pricing stock issue items, the same set of instructions would apply to each item and this cyclical process would continue until all items had been processed.

(b) *Unconditional jumps.* This diverts to an instruction out of sequence and does so automatically and without choice. If, as in (a) above a series of instructions have to be carried out on every data item, the control will direct back to a previous instruction to enable the cycle to be repeated.

(c) *Conditional jump.* This occurs when alternative courses of action present themselves and a decision must be made which to follow. The criterion upon which judgement is made will be the testing of some quality in the data item. If, for example, in the stock pricing process mentioned in (a) 15 % discount was to be deducted for all items over £100, then the question Is more than £100? would be asked of each data item; the answer 'Yes' resulting in a different course of action to answer 'No'. In other words, the next instruction executed in the total program sequence would be conditional on the result of the test applied.

(d) *Arithmetic.* This embraces all of the mathematical operations demanded of the program, such as Add, Multiply, Subtract, Divide and compare.

One further principle must be mentioned in this review of programming—*address modification.* In discussing the basic format of a program instruction, that is, operation and operand, it could be inferred that such a detailed instruction is necessary for every item of data dealt with by the program. If this were so it would present us with a rather ludicrous situation. Say, for example, 1 000 records had to be read into store, then sticking rigidly to this principle a series of instructions something like this would have to be completed.

$$
\begin{array}{llllll}
\text{Read record and store in} & & & & & 1601 \\
\text{''} & \text{''} & \text{''} & \text{''} & \text{''} & 1602 \\
\text{''} & \text{''} & \text{''} & \text{''} & \text{''} & 1603 \\
\\
\text{''} & \text{''} & \text{''} & \text{''} & \text{''} & 2600
\end{array}
$$

This, of course, is a far too laborious a procedure and indeed very wasteful of computer storage space. In a situation like this the address held in the instruction register can be automatically modified to give the next address required without the need to store a separate instruction. This is done by inserting a modifier in a register which, when added to the original operand address will give the next operand location.

The above is only one example of this technique and in this case, having stored the first address 1601, on completion of the operation 1 is inserted into the modifying register which when added to 1601 gives the next address 1602. This process is repeated, adding 1 to the modifier as each cycle is completed.

EXERCISES

1. What do you understand by the term 'machine code'? Show how programs, once they are written, can be prepared in a form acceptable for storage in a computer.

2. Give an account of the advantages and the disadvantages that accrue to the use of application packages.

3. Describe the functions of an operating system.

4. What do you understand by 'utility software'. Suggest some of the purposes for which this is used.

5. Argue the case for the use of low level languages in program construction as opposed to the use of high level languages.

6. What do you understand by a program loop? Give an example of its use from a routine with which you are familiar.

7. Draw a flowchart illustrating the principles of:
        (a) An unconditional jump.
        (b) A conditional jump.
        (c) A loop.

8. What do you understand by an Operation and an Operand in connection with a program instruction. Describe how these two elements are dealt with in the central processor.

9. One of the functions of an operating system is to communicate with the computer operator. Give examples of the type of messages you would expect such a system to generate.

10

Systems Considerations

The question 'What is a System?' is not easily answered in a few words. Research through reference books and dictionaries will reveal a fairly varied set of definitions from which it is possible to extract some fundamental common factors. These will be looked at in this chapter. Within the context of Data Processing Systems possibly the nearest definition we can get is 'An ordered set of procedures designed to organise, motivate, monitor and control an activity or series of activities to accomplish a pre-determined purpose.'

From a semantics point of view, different schools of thought are evident in interpreting what is understood by the word *system*. One would have it that there is only one total universal system embracing all physical and human organisation and activity and that defined areas of activity are sub-systems within this. Another will look at it from an organisational viewpoint and suggest that the activities of an organisation as a whole are the system, and that manufacturing activities, sales activities, data processing activities, and so on, are sub-sets within the overall system.

As a basis of this discussion on systems considerations we will take a 'system' as referring to a discrete area of processing activity as one would generally find to fall within the spectrum of normal commercial usage, such as a stock control system, a wages system, a sales ledger system. However, this with the reservation that such 'systems' do not operate in isolation and they will have an inter-relationship with each other. In addition, the 'systems' to a greater or lesser degree will in some aspects be integrated with each other, and will operate within the same general business structure and work towards the same common purpose, i.e. that of the organisation as a whole.

SYSTEMS ENVIRONMENT

A data processing system does not exist just for the joy of being there. It exists as a result of some other primary activity, manufacturing, servicing, research and so on, and its purpose in life is to record, control, promote and sometimes organise that activity.

The activity that it seeks to serve, will have a bearing on the environment within which the system works. Such environmental factors can be considered under two main headings, *physical* and *organisational.*

Physical environment

This, in the first place, will be determined within the context of the way in which these activities are organised. The structure of the system will be influenced by such factors as:

(a) Are business activities concentrated into one location, or are activities dispersed over geographically widely separated units involving in the latter case possibly a complex system of inter-communications?
(b) How is data emanating from the activities originated, how is it fed into the processing system?
(c) What response time is demanded from the processing system to provide the level of control called for?

It is suggested that these factors will have a material bearing on the siting of a computer and whether one large central installation, a number of smaller inter-connected configurations, or satellites of a central machine would best serve the needs of the organisation. Data transmission questions may well have to be asked with the resultant possible desirability of remote interrogation facilities. Arising from the provision of such terminals the operating mode of the computer and provision of relevant hardware will be a major systems consideration.

In the second place we will be concerned with the physical environment within which the actual data processing activities take place. As experience has often shown, there is frequently a matter of compromise between fitting hardware and personnel into modified existing accommodation rather than new tailor made premises. A number of factors are worthy of consideration in providing the environmental conditions that will promote an efficient working unit.

Many of the considerations will be fairly self evident i.e., lighting, heating, noise control, minimum working areas etc. Some of these will be mandatory within the framework of Shops, Offices and Railway Premises Acts. There are further important considerations when designing the accommodation in which a computer department will work; these are:

1. An arrangement to facilitate a logical flow of work through the system and at the same time minimise the distances over which work has to be carried.

2. The provision of pleasing working conditions and rest areas, bearing in mind the repetitive and often boring work in data preparation procedures, punching cards or tape and encoding MICR documents.
3. Provision of the support services to ensure conditions essential to the efficient working of the machines, air conditioning, temperature, humidity and dust control.
4. Adequate facilities for supervision and control of both machines and data.
5. Security of access to machine rooms and stores and also of confidential records and potentially valuable documents such as cheque blanks.
6. Provision of facilities for machine maintenance staff.
7. Where direct access to the computer or to off-line data preparation equipment is used, the provision of an adequate communications network.
8. Controlled environment facilities for off-line storage of files held on magnetic media.
9. Provision of adequate office accommodation for management, systems design, programming and operating staff.

Organisational environment

By definition, no automatic data processing system is an end in itself. It exists in relation to stimuli applied to it and information emanating from it in relation to the structure and objectives of the organisation for which it provides a service. It is essentially part of the mechanics of a service that exists to provide information at the right time, in the right form and in the right place, promoting and guiding the controlling mechanism of the organisation. This it does by monitoring, recording and processing data related to the activities with which the organisation is involved. It will, for example, provide information to guide management policy decisions, to control production activities and to optimise the use of available resources.

While it is not practical to lay down hard and fast rules, and indeed exceptions will spring to mind particularly in the case of direct entry of source data through terminal devices, nevertheless a data processing system can be looked at in three defined stages.

1. Operations before entry to computer system.
2. Computer operations.
3. Operations arising from computer output reports.

The first stage could well include originating, collating, checking, editing source data, and the third implementation of action or policy based on output reporting.

A system can, from one point of view, be looked at as a cyclical process that is in the long term determined by and in the short term influenced by the activities taking place in the environment within which it is situated. By the same token, the information generated by the system will in turn determine and influence the activities of which the system is the subject.

At this point we can well ask ourselves, should the organisational environment determine the format of the system within which it works, or should the format of the system generate its own organisational environment. In practice, the solution usually falls somewhere between the two. The process of analysis of existing procedures and

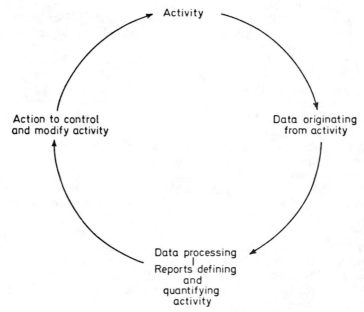

Figure 10.1. Cyclical representation of system

systems design does not necessarily sweep away the old completely nor does it necessarily introduce a system to exclusively fit into the present order of things. It will seek, retaining where desirable, present procedures and introducing where necessary new or revised procedures, to formulate a system that within the framework of available resources, will provide the most adequate service.

We saw earlier that an automated data processing system is not an end in itself. It is true to say that no data processing system exists in isolation, but will be related to and interlinked at some points with other systems operating in the same environment. The process of completely integrating 'systems' as we are thinking of them, into one overall system within the organisation, 'the system', is a complex problem not easily solved and the principle not easily implemented.

When we examine the matter it becomes evident that many data records are relevant to and can be used within more than one procedure. For example, a statement of number of hours worked by an operative could be used in (a) the calculation of wages, (b) a costing procedure and (c) as a basis for the apportionment of overheads. In theory there is no need for this statement to be recorded three times, once for each system, and providing general access to it is available, then the one record is sufficient. This is really the beginning of an approach to an integrated system.

Of course, such an approach tends to cut across traditional department boundaries—the wages office—the cost office—the accounts office—all operating their different systems but using in many cases the same records. Indeed, since, for example, the basic movement records for a sales order processing system are the same as are used for up-dating a stock inventory system and, in turn, the stock inventory records are the base for a purchase order system which in turn provides records to up-date the stock inventory system, why then keep the systems in watertight compartments.

If we intend this principle to embrace all information processing systems within the organisation then, of course, this pre-supposes that there must be available a comprehensive store of all data records, available for all the procedures in which they are required. Such an assembly of the total data generated is usually known as a *data base*. In other words, we are building up a set of files that are systems independent. Naturally, bearing in mind the range of procedures for which such records will be required such files would have to be of a direct access type.

SYSTEMS STRUCTURE

A system, within the terms we are considering in this chapter, can be broken down into a number of sub-divisions as follows:

System.
Sub-systems.
Procedures.
Operations.
Tasks.

Of these, a task is the smallest unit of work we can identify within a system. For example, we may find this structure evident in a manual sales ledger system as shown in Figure 10.2.

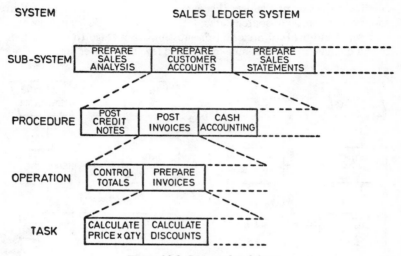

Figure 10.2. Systems breakdown

While a breakdown of this nature may not be as evident in a computer processed system, there are nevertheless defined work stages within the system, although to identify them in terms of this terminology may be neither useful or practical. The structure of such a system could well incorporate the following stages:

1. Preparation of source data manually in the form of a despatch note identifying customer and goods supplied.
2. Preparation of this data in a machine acceptable form such as punched cards.
3. A series of computer runs to locate items, calculate values, insert discounts and generally provide an expanded file containing invoice details.
4. A print run to produce hard copy invoices for despatch to customers.
5. Master file up-dating runs to provide full Sales Ledger detail and current balances.
6. Periodically a master file print-out to provide customer sales statements.

The existence of these procedural levels within the system are not so apparent as in a manual system. It could be argued that the master files represent the apex of the system, the production of invoices a sub-system, the processes concerned with inserting prices and calculating values a procedure, the data preparation stage an operation and the preparation of source data a task. Such a classification, however, represents more of a horizontal progression from stage to stage rather than a detailed heirarchial breakdown into levels of procedure.

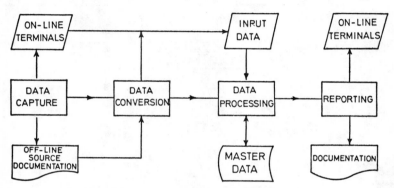

Figure 10.3. Progression of information through system

As suggested previously, a system can be regarded as being structured in three main sections (a) the data origination and preparation stage, (b) the machine processing stage and (c) the output reporting stage. The detailed structure within these stages is normally the subject of a systems specification. However, the main areas within such a structure can be summarised as follows:

(a) The collection, vetting and batching of source data. Its transmission to the data processing department and its validation and control. Its conversion where necessary into a machine readable form.

(b) Initial definition of computer run procedures and programs. Creation of master files. Reading current data from (a) to movement files. Computer up-dating procedures. Procedures for extracting and reporting information.

(c) Procedures for distributing output reports and procedures for taking action on these.

SYSTEMS RESOURCES

The resources necessary to implement and operate a data processing system can be classified under five main headings:

> Machine resources.
> Human resources.
> Software resources.
> Information resources.
> Control resources.

Indeed, the viability of the system will depend on the presence, the interaction and the quality of all these.

Machine resources

We have seen earlier that a system can be broken down into an input sub-system, a processing sub-system and a reporting sub-system. Machine resources will fall into these categories. While it would be impractical to give an exhaustive list of all of the machines that could possibly be used in operating a system, and in any case the main ones have been mentioned in some detail elsewhere, the following is a brief summary:

Input:	Punched card and punched paper tape preparation equipment.
	Remote on-line terminals.
	Readers—punched media, MICR and OCR.
	Key to tape magnetic encoders.
Processing:	Central processing unit.
	Backing storage—Magnetic media.
Output:	Line and character printers.
	Graph plotters.
	Visual display units.
	Microfilm.
	Punched media—cards and tape.
	Ancillary handling equipment—bursters, decollators, trimmers, guillotines, folding, addressing, envelope insertion, franking machines.

Human resources

Perhaps the most important resource consideration is the expertise and experience of the personnel responsible for and engaged in running

the system. Falling into fairly well defined categories these are
(a) Data processing management staff.
(b) Systems analysis and design staff.
(c) Programmers.
(d) Computer operators.
(e) Data preparation and document handling staff.
(f) Data reception and control staff.
(g) Library and file maintenance staff.
(h) Maintenance personnel.

All the above will work within the data processing department, but as an integral part of the system we must include staff occupied in recording source data and indeed the users of the output reports.

Software resources

Under this heading we can include all these factors that control the operation of the hardware and cause it to effect those procedures demanded of the system.

(a) Application programs.
(b) Compilers and assemblers for generating object programs.
(c) Utility programs for carrying out standard routines.
(d) Operation systems.

Information resources

This represents the whole range of data that is the subject of the system.

(a) Source data arising directly from the activity the system is designed to record and control.
(b) Input records prepared from source data.
(c) Systems files containing master data.
(d) Files containing static reference data.
(e) Output reports.

Control resources

To define how the system should operate, the safeguards to be imposed on the system for accuracy and security and to ensure that the system objectives are realised.

SYSTEMS DEFINITION

A systems definition, or specification is that collection of documents which formally specifies in detail how the system will be operated, and will be made available in whole or in part to personnel who are involved at any stage of the system. Its object is not so much to provide a general guide and explanation of the system as to set down in a fine degree of detail the procedures that must be adopted. It will usually contain a number of sections:

1. A statement of systems objectives.
2. A description of the system.
3. Document specifications.
4. File specifications.
5. Specification of output.
6. Hardware requirements.
7. Program specification.
8. Implementation procedures.

Systems objectives

This section will define what the system is designed to accomplish. It will make reference to the major procedures covered by the system and, in broad terms, the information these procedures will generate. It will probably outline any organisational changes in departments effected by the introduction of the system and will enumerate the benefits accruing from these changes under the following headings:

(a) Improvements in output information in terms of both quality and timeliness.
(b) Improved use of resources both human and machine.
(c) Better control facilities.
(d) Financial advantages resulting directly from the changeover to computer processing and indirectly through the realisation of (a), (b) and (c).

Description of the system

This will cover all of the main procedures within the system from the preparation of source data to the final output of reports. The description will be sectionalised as follows:

(a) *Data capture.* The routine for recording data at source. A specification of the forms used to record data. How data is to be transmitted or forwarded to the data processing section. Controls that are to be imposed to ensure accuracy and security.
(b) *Data preparation procedures.* How data is to be converted to machine input form. The design of input documents. The flow of data through the preparation process, verification and other control

procedures. Deadlines for the availability of prepared data for processing purposes, and controls to ensure that all data has been assembled.

(c) *Computer procedures.* Flow-charts of procedures should be suitably annotated with explanatory notes where necessary. The programs applicable to each run and the files that are to be used should be specified.

(d) *Clerical procedures.* Under this heading all of the documentation involved in controlling and monitoring the system will be specified. While this will vary from situation to situation it will include records of receipt of source documentation, compilation of control totals for reconciliation at varying stages in the system, logging use of data and program files. In fact all those clerical records that are a necessary adjunct to the effective operation of the systems.

(e) *Output procedures.* The form output reports will take, the number of copies required, to whom they will be distributed, and special security problems associated with reports.

Document specification

Specimen copies of all documents used in the system should be included in a systems definition file together with detailed notes on how they should be completed and the circumstances under which they should be used. The number of copies that are to be prepared and what should be done with each copy.

File specification

The format of file records must be specified in complete detail with record layout diagrams defining each data field. Files must be named, the sequence of records on the file defined and the contents of file labels specified.

Output specification

Illustrations of output format should be supplied bearing in mind that the user's requirements should be taken into consideration in this design. For printed output detailed print layout charts should be prepared, showing the print positions that will be occupied by data fields.

Hardware requirements

This will identify the equipment and machines needed to run the system. This should include not only computer hardware but data preparation equipment and devices required for dealing with computer output.

Program specification

This must be prepared in the complete detail necessary for a programmer to write the required programs. Flowcharts will be included at both outline and detailed levels together with supporting documentation to ensure a detailed and unambiguous statement of programming requirements.

Implementation procedures

It is usual to include in a systems specification details of the plans to implement the system. Particular attention will be paid to procedures for setting up the system, introduction of new documentation, work flow, file creation, development of control techniques etc. The changeover method will be defined, for example pilot or parallel running, and, where relevant, measures for proving the system by comparing results with existing procedures.

While there is no standard way of drawing up a systems specification and its detail will vary from application to application. The basic intention is to provide a fully comprehensive and documented account of the system that will:

(a) Provide a medium for the maintenance of standards.
(b) Provide an account of the means for achieving the objectives of the system.
(c) Mitigate the problems of staff changeover.
(d) Provide the means of increasing the security and accuracy of records.
(e) Provide a channel of communication between all those people in any way involved in the system.

SYSTEMS MAINTENANCE

A system once having been designed and implemented is not necessarily going to remain unchanged for ever. Indeed, in natural processes of business activity changes will occur that will give rise to a demand for modifications to the system. These changes may on the one hand have major implications, or, on the other hand, they may be just minor adjustments to the system. To list all the factors giving rise to change in a commercial situation is impossible but among those fairly frequently met are:

(a) Introduction of new processing equipment involving a drastic change in processing method. For example, a stock control system changing from batch processing to a real-time mode.

(b) Changes in user requirements to meet the needs of a changing market.

(c) Variance in volumes of data. It is not always possible to accurately forecast trends in volume. Exceptional circumstances may arise to give a sudden and dramatic increase in the activity giving rise to the data.

(d) Changes in product range leading to modifications to coding systems and possibly to record format to accommodate new descriptions.

(e) Organisational changes, for example a change of company ownership leading to a need for systems to conform with other companies within a group.

(f) Changes arising out of proved inadequacies in the system.

While it is difficult to envisage a situation where a system would have to be scrapped in its entirety, changes of the nature mentioned above will give rise to modifications of a greater or smaller degree becoming necessary to the system. It is easy to say that when a system is constructed it should have built into it a degree of flexibility that will accommodate change. The problem arises in deciding what degree of flexibility is acceptable since any degree tends to be wasteful. To design a record format, for example, that would accommodate any possible increase in record length could represent a very uneconomic use of storage space.

A system, however, should be designed bearing in mind that modifications will become necessary in the process of time and should be sufficiently flexible to accommodate minor modifications easily without causing a major upheaval. For example, coding systems should be flexible enough to accommodate new groupings, data record formats to accommodate minor changes, the parameters of validity checks capable of adjustment to meet a changing situation. Minor procedural changes can be more easily made if programs are written on a modular basis so that a module can be modified in isolation.

Perhaps the essence of systems maintenance is system review. While some situations by virtue of their explosive nature will make themselves immediately felt, it is the regular review in the light of user requirements that will ensure the system maintains its planned objective, that of providing an effective service.

SYSTEMS PHILOSOPHY

It could be said that, fundamentally, a system exists to effect change. Change in the structure of the raw material it receives and change in the structure of the activities it monitors through the feedback of control information. In this it is analagous to a manufacturing situation where raw materials are processed, components brought together and a finished product fabricated in accordance with a pre-determined plan and design.

The factors that will be present to these ends are:

Detailed planning and design.

An effective organisation of work flow.

Product monitoring to ensure quality control.

Careful specification of raw materials to ensure their suitability for the job.

Effecting processes in the most economic way consistent with the required quality of the end product.

The supply and efficient use of tools and machines.

Design geared to meet market demands.

A working environment in which these factors can take place to the best advantage.

An organisational environment which seeks to guide, control and generally co-ordinate these activities.

Similarly, in a data processing system, accepting source data as its raw material and producing an end product to meet the needs of the user, the same factors will apply.

EXERCISES

1. What do you understand by an 'integrated system'? Describe how a data record of your choice could be used in a number of different procedures.

2. Describe briefly the hardware resources that you feel are necessary for a sales ledger system, operated in a batch processing mode and designed to print out statements of account at the end of each month.

3. Under what main headings would you expect information to be assembled in a systems specification?

4. What do you understand by 'systems maintenance'? Give examples of situations that may arise leading to a need to modify a system.

5. Outline the main environmental conditions that you would have to concern yourself with when planning to implement a new computer department.

6. It is generally considered there are three defined stages in a data processing system. Give a short account of each of these.

11

File Organisation

First of all, it is necessary to remind ourselves of the basic principles previously considered:

1. A computer file is a collection of related records each uniquely identifiable by its key.
2. Both records and the data items they contain may be of fixed or variable length in character.
3. For processing purposes records must be transferred to computer store and then, on completion of the procedure, back again to file.
4. The unit of transfer between file and processor is usually known as a block, or in some cases a bucket, and that this unit may contain one or more records.

In this chapter discussion will be limited to two file media: magnetic tape and magnetic disc. These are the two most generally used for backing storage, and, indeed, many of the principles relating to locating, retrieving and processing records held on disc are equally applicable to drum and card types of direct access store.

In planning the organisation of records on a file, a number of factors will be taken into consideration, although they are not all necessarily relevant to any particular file media. The significance of these factors which are listed below will become more apparent throughout this chapter.

Anticipated number of records in file.
Format of records—to what degree variable or fixed length.
Anticipated maximum length of records.
Record identification.
Record location on file.
Sequence of records on file.
Security of information.
File maintenance.
File up-dating procedures.
Record retrieval.

One further point before we look at the two file media under consideration. The terms *serial, sequential* and *random* are used universally to define the order in which records are held but the interpretation of the first of these is not always consistent. For the purpose of this chapter, the term *serial* will be used to denote a processing order rather than a record order. In other words where processing follows the sequence of hardware locations irrespective of the key of the record stored in them (Figure 11.1).

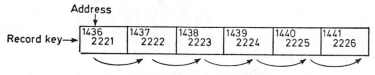

Figure 11.1. Schematic serial processing

Sequential processing will be taken to mean the processing of records in sequence of their key irrespective of the address of the location in which they are stored (Figure 11.2). Random processing used for the situation where records, whether they be stored in a defined sequence or not, are directly accessible irrespective of the preceeding or succeeding location address or record key.

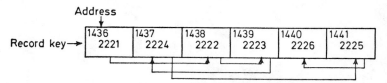

Figure 11.2. Schematic sequential processing

MAGNETIC TAPE

We have already seen that records on tape are stored, one after each other along the length of the tape and, if they are variable in length, their limits and the limits of their constituent parts are defined by markers; although the limits of fixed length records can be defined by a character and field count. Blocks of data for movement to and from the processor are identified by an end of block marker and separated by an inter-block gap. Furthermore, location of any particular record is by serial search through the tape by transferring successive blocks to store until the record sought is identified.

It will be appreciated that if records are required for processing in an order other than that in which stored, such a serial search for individual records would take an unacceptable length of time. For file processing, therefore, records are invariably held on tape in key sequence order which means, in this case, serial and sequential processing are synonymous. It will be evident, of course, that location addresses are not necessary, and indeed would be meaningless on a magnetic tape.

To modify records as they stand on a reel of tape is, of course, impractical as any change in a record would overwrite the existing record. Also, any shortening of a record would leave a residue of the original and any lengthening of a record would overwrite part of the following record. There is no room between records to insert additions in sequence order.

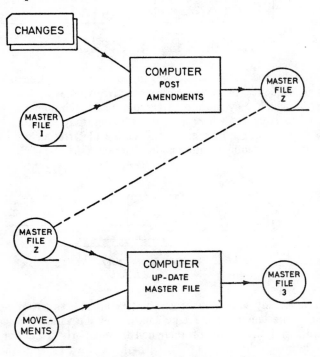

Figure 11.3. Updating tape with changes and movement

Nevertheless, tape files have to be maintained, which means the addition, deletion and amendment of records. Records have to be up-dated with movement data which, in many cases will increase the record length. The way round this problem is to hold, on separate tapes, change records for file maintenance and movement records for file up-dating, and sort these into the same sequence as the records on the master tape. Blocks of records are moved from master tape to store where the records are amended and updated with the new data, and the revised record in turn written out to a new tape. Figure 11.3 illustrates a file up-dating procedure from movement records held on tape, and a maintenance run from changes held on punched card.

By and large, tape file systems are only suitable for batch processing procedures where quantities of movement data can be assembled sequentially and applied in one run to master records held in the same sequence on another tape. These files are not suitable for up-dating individual records at random.

MAGNETIC DISCS

In contrast to a magnetic tape which provides one continuous recording surface, the recording areas on magnetic discs are physically segregated and their recording capacity defined. Having located one end of a tape, progression through its length is automatic while the separate recording areas on a disc, cylinders, tracks and sectors have to be positively located. To make location possible, a system of addressing is demanded by allocating to each recording area a unique reference.

A survey of all the addressing systems used in all the various types of disc systems would be impossible in one book, but we can illustrate the principle through one example. It was seen in Chapter 7 that a disc

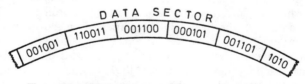

Figure 11.4. Section of disc track holding 6-bit words

surface contains a number of concentric recording tracks. In most systems each track is divided into a number of recording sectors or blocks of a standard size (say, holding 512 characters) and data is recorded linearly in bits along the track (see Figure 11.4). File records are organised in cylinder format, that is, in a vertical array of tracks.

If we wish to address down to block level within each individual track, two references are required (a) to identify the track, and (b) to identify the sector within the track. To accomplish this, in systems using physical track divisions into blocks, a second recording area just before the commencement of each block contains its address within the track (see Figure 11.5).

The next level of addressing is at track level and here two alternatives present themselves. Either to number up tracks on each surface sequentially from the perimeter to the centre of the disc, or to number them vertically in terms of disc surfaces.

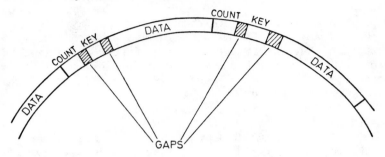

Count area holds address of following data sector.
Key area holds control data and identification key
of record stored in data sector.

Figure 11.5. Blocks in tracks

Since, as we have seen, records are stored in cylinder format, it is preferable to adopt the latter method. This means that all tracks on the first recording surface could, for example, be numbered '0', the second surface, 1, the third surface 2 and so on. On a six disc pack with ten recording surfaces, tracks within a vertical recording cylinder will have addresses 0-9. The track address is inserted on the track itself for control purposes.

Cylinders are addressed by virtue of the order of tracks in the horizontal plane of the disc surface, the outermost track numbered say 0 and the track nearest the disc centre 99. This is illustrated in Figure 11.6. The final level of addressing is of course when a multiple number of disc transport are connected on-line to the computer and the disc file containing the records to be referenced has to be identified.

Levels of address can then be summarised as follows:

Disc transport unit.	By electronic switching by control element of central processor.
Recording cylinder.	By control instruction to access mechanism moving read/write head arms to locate specified cylinder.
Recording track.	By head switching—that is 'turning on' the head located adjacent to the track sought.
Recording block, sector or bucket.	By disc rotation and search until required recording area is located.

Having seen how any specific hardware recording area on disc can be located, and since stored records will be identified by their key, there remains the problem of associating a record key with a hardware address. That is to say, ascertaining in which hardware location a specific record is stored.

This process is known as *indexing*. The method used will depend on the order, if any, in which records are stored and will also take into account the levels of addressing that we have just reviewed.

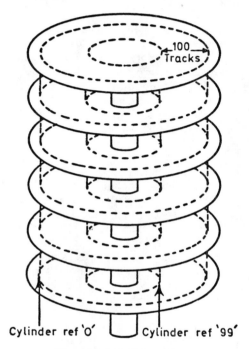

Figure 11.6. Cylinder addresses

For example, as two extremes, the following examples may illustrate these principles. A sales ledger system involving 1999 ledger cards serially numbered with customer account numbers 0-1999 may be filed in numerical order in two boxes numbered 0 and 1. Each box sub-divided into 10 sections labelled 0-9 and cards in each section segregated into groups of 10 by tag cards also labelled 0-9.

Behind each tag card are 10 ledger cards in numeric order. In such a filing system the location address of each card will be synonymous with the card key number. Ledger record card 1467 will be the seventh card behind the sixth tag in the fourth section of box number one. Its address in effect is 1467.

If, on the other hand, we wished to refer to a specific phrase in a specific book in a library we would first of all identify the subject section of the library, then the individual book, then the page number followed by the line in the page. If we wanted to keep a written reference to enable us to easily trace the phrase in future it would be in terms of subject reference, book reference, page number and line number.

In the first case, the indexing system is based on a direct relationship between location address reference and a reference contained in and identifying the record. In the second case no such relationship exists. Translated in terms of storage, on the one hand we may have records whose key sequence is identical to the location sequence in which they are stored and on the other hand records whose sequence of keys bears no relation to the location addresses. In the first case records are stored sequentially in consecutive storage locations; in the second case they are stored at random in no particular address order.

ALLOCATION OF FILE STORAGE AREAS

It is usual to allocate a defined area of storage for each file in terms of cylinders. For example, a sales ledger file might be allocated cylinders 23-48. It was seen earlier that several factors must be borne in mind when deciding on the size of area required. Two important factors will, of course, be the number of records and their length. However, by the nature of things, many files tend to expand in the course of time through the insertion of new records and the increased length of individual records through updating, and so space must be allowed in the allocated area for this expansion. How this is dealt with in practice we will see later in this chapter.

On direct access file devices there are a number of ways in which files can be organised. These are (a) serial, (b) sequential, (c) indexed sequential and (d) direct.

SERIAL FILE ORGANISATION

The principle used here is to store records in key sequence order in consecutive storage locations, rather similar to the principles adopted for magnetic tape (Figure 11.7). A fixed number of records are allocated to each track and, in a system where tracks are sub-divided physically into a number of sectors or blocks, each block may contain only one record or, to make greatest advantage of available storage

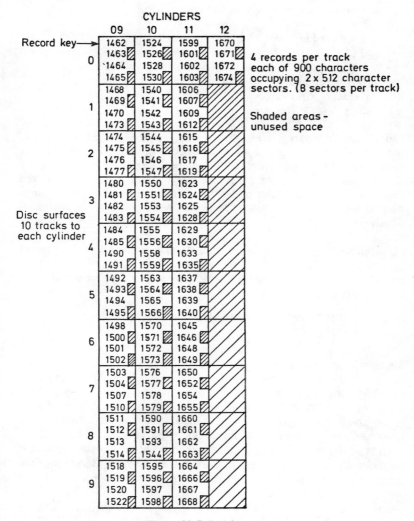

Figure 11.7. Serial storage

space, records may be 'BLOCKED', that is, a fixed number fitted into each block. Since read/write commands will only operate down to block level, all the records in an individual block will be transferred to storage where the particular record required will be identified.

File records are then stored as follows:

> 1st record in 1st block of 1st track in 1st cylinder.
> 2nd „   „ 2nd „   „   „   „   „   „   „
> 9th record in 1st block of 2nd track in 1st cylinder.
> 10th „   „ 2nd „   „   „   „   „   „   „
> 81st record in 1st block of 1st track of 2nd cylinder.
> 82nd „   „ 2nd „   „   „   „   „   „   „

and so on. Of course, if more than one record is stored in a block, then records, say, 1 and 2 are stored in 1st block of 1st track of 1st cylinder and this pattern of distribution continued.

Now, while in this mode of file organisation records are stored sequentially in consecutive addresses, processing follows the sequence of locations rather than the sequence of records which has two main disadvantages.

(a) It does not permit the insertion of new records in their correct place in the sequence.
(b) It does not permit the expansion of a record beyond the fixed storage space allocated.

In both events a complete rewrite of the file will be necessary.

Sequential processing

This form of file organisation will meet the two objections stated above. In this case, processing follows the sequence of record keys irrespective of their address. In the interests of economy in storage space and in optimising processing speed, records would initially be organised as suggested in serial processing above (Figure 11.7).

If it becomes necessary to insert a record within the sequence, it is stored in the overflow section of the file area. A tag is inserted into the home track immediately after the record with the preceding key quoting the address at which the inserted record is to be found. At this point processing is diverted from a serial progression through locations to the next sequential key. In the same way, a record that has outgrown its storage space will be moved to an overflow area and a re-directing tag inserted. Of course, the insertion of tags pre-supposes that there is room for them in the home track. If this is not so, then the preceding record in key sequence is moved to the overflow area to make room for it and an additional tag inserted giving its new address (Figure 11.8).

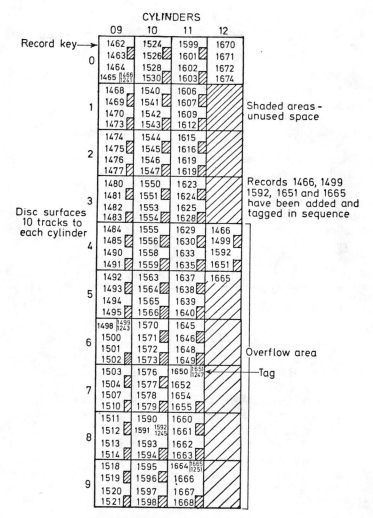

Figure 11.8. Tagging principle

Files organised serially and sequentially are generally used in a search mode of access. This means, in an up-dating run, movement records are sorted into the same sequence, both sets of records read sequentially into the CPU in blocks, where record keys are compared for a match. Where matching takes place the file record is up-dated and the revised record written back to its original location on disc over-writing the original record. Of course, records for which no matching movement data exists are similarly written back, but in an unchanged form.

Sequential processing is very fast and efficient providing a substantial proportion of the records have matching movement records and are up-dated. This factor, known as the 'HIT RATE' is said to be high when a large proportion of records are up-dated and low when only a few are processed. It will be appreciated that processing with a low hit rate is uneconomic because a large number of records will be transferred to the processor, go through a matching routine and be transferred back unaltered.

Given then a file media that provides direct access facilities, it is desirable in a low hit rate situation to take advantage of this facility even though records may be organised sequentially. This cannot be done unless the physical location of each record is known which in turn means some kind of Address/Record Key indexing system. Files organised in a serial or sequential processing mode can lend themselves, within the limits of the coding system used, to generating record keys in a fairly simple form of index known as self-indexing.

Self indexing

If, for example, cylinders 36-45 were allocated to hold a given file then, discounting space reserved for control information, the address of the 1st record could be stated as 3600. That is, in cylinder 36 the 1st track = 0 and the first block in the track = 0. All we have to do is to allocate 3600 as the key to the first record and follow this principle through the sequence of records and we have what is known as a self-indexing direct addressing system.

However, of course, this direct relationship does not apply if more than one record is located in each block. In this case a record key coding can be devised which will, on the application of a simple arithmetic process, generate the address of the record. Assuming four records to a block then, as an illustration, we could have the following situation:

BLOCK LOCATION 3600 holds records 14400, 14401, 14402, 14403
     ,,   ,,   3601 ,,   ,,   14404, 14405, 14406, 14407
     ,,   ,,   3602 ,,   ,,   14408, 14409, 14410, 14411
     ,,   ,,   3603 ,,   ,,   14412, 14413, 14414, 14415

It is then a simple process of dividing the record key by the blocking factor, 4, to obtain the hardware address.

The address of record 14410 is $\frac{14410}{4} = 3602$

While this self addressing technique appears a simple and logical approach to the problem there are major difficulties which often make its use in commercial data processing systems undesirable.

(a) It pre-supposes an unbroken sequence of record keys. This rarely happens in practice. Gaps will occur, for example, when records are deleted leading to a poor utilisation of store space as locations must be allocated to every key in the sequence.

(b) There may not be room for the insertion of tags when a fixed blocking factor is used, and in any case the insertion of records in sequence will upset the arithmetic address generation principle.

(c) The example given above is a fairly simple one to illustrate the underlying principle. In practice, the location address may involve a large group of digits and the record key may have to conform with some other coding criteria. Indeed, it may be mixed Alpha/Numeric. Under these circumstances it could be very difficult to formulate an address generating formula.

However, self indexing does combine with the advantages of sequential processing a facility for direct access.

Indexed sequential organisation

This is an indexing system that seeks to overcome the short-comings of self-indexing by providing a method of locating the address of records even though no affinity exists between the location address and the record key, and is therefore suitable for any key-coding system. It, nevertheless, still works on the principle as the name suggests, that the records are stored sequentially.

It is based on a hierarchial structure of search levels, the highest being a search to locate the disc unit, assuming more than one, the next level the cylinder within the unit, and the next the track within the cylinder. It works in principle as follows:

(a) An index is held in store listing the highest key number held on each unit against the unit number.

Unit level index

Highest key	Unit number
19672	1
37846	2
56231	3

If it is required for instance to locate the record with key 20389 then by comparison with the listed highest keys, the nearest one above is selected directing the search to the relevant unit.

(b) Within the unit a section of store will be allocated to hold an index listing the highest key held on each cylinder against the cylinder reference.

Cylinder level index

Highest key	Cylinder number
19965	1
20163	2
20473	3
20714	4
37582	99
37846	100

Again by comparison with highest keys, the one nearest above 20389 is selected and the next level of search directed to that cylinder, in this example cylinder 3.

(c) The cylinder will hold in store an index listing highest key number on each track against the track numbers.

Track level index

Highest key	Track number
20194	1
20236	2
20261	3
20298	4
20331	5
20362	6
20394	7
20410	8
20443	9
20473	10

A further comparison of key number with highest track key index will direct search to track 7 where a search through the track will locate record 20389.

A diagram showing the total searching routine is given in Figure 11.9.

The description above takes the addressing level down to a track. This is not always the case, as some disc systems use a variable format

147

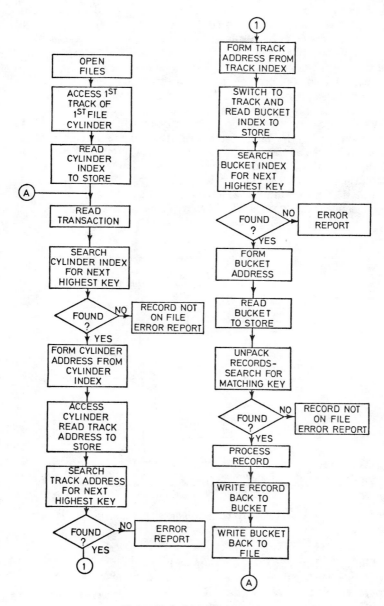

Figure 11.9. Searching routine

track and others as we have seen are physically divided into sectors, often known as buckets. Should this be the case, addressing could well extend down to bucket level by a further bucket index. A bucket containing possibly a number of records is read into store where the record sought will be identified by reference to its key.

There remains the problem of the treatment of overflow records in an indexed sequential file. Techniques for this vary from system to system so it is only practical to outline here some basic ideas.

When a storage area is allocated to contain a file it is often divided into three parts. The bulk of the area in which the initial records are placed is known as the home area, a track or a number of buckets are left empty on each cylinder to accept records that will be added to the file during its life, this is known as a cylinder overflow area, and a third area at the end of the file is left empty as a reserve should cylinder areas become full, this is known as an independent overflow area.

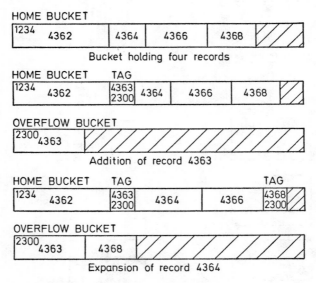

Figure 11.10. Treatment of bucket overflow .

While, in theory, record insertion and expansion could be dealt with by leaving sufficient unoccupied space in the bucket, in practice this would be a very wasteful procedure and still give no guarantee that overflow conditions would not occur.

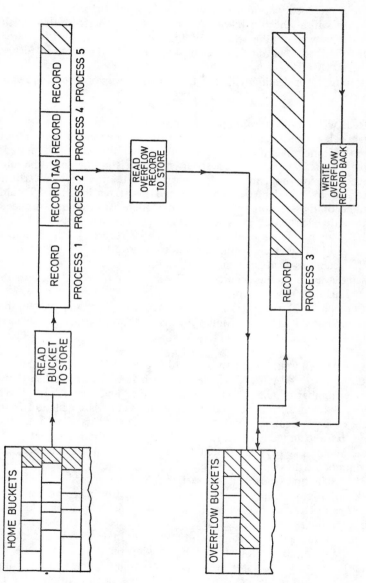

Figure 11.11. Processing overflow records

The technique most commonly adopted is the insertion of tags to identify the location of overflow records. The tag, inserted in key sequence within the block will quote the key of the record to which it refers as well as the address of the location in the overflow area where the record will be found. This technique is illustrated in Figure 11.10.

A routine for dealing with overflow areas can involve the following steps:

1. Read whole bucket into input area of store.
2. Unpack records and process sequentially matching with input records and up-dating records as necessary. If no tag encountered, read bucket back to store overwriting existing records. Should records have expanded to an overflow situation move overflow record to cylinder overflow area and insert tag in block. Should none of these records need up-dating, there is, of course, no need to write back to disc as existing data remains unchanged.
3. If a tag is encountered the processing of records in the block is interrupted while control is directed to the overflow record location, the record is read into the input section of store, processed in the same way as home records in (2) above and moved back to its original overflow location.
4. Control then goes back to the next record or tag in sequence in the home bucket and so continues in this way until the whole bucket is processed (see Figure 11.11).

One or two points need to be guarded against in using this method of dealing with overflow. The file can reach a point where a disproportionate number of tags are inserted into home buckets which leads to a material slowing down of processing rate as records are called in from the overflow area. Another relevant consideration is that both the home bucket and the overflow record may be in the input section of store simultaneously. Sufficient store space must be allocated to accommodate these.

It is sometimes possible to insert an additional record in the home bucket if room has previously been made for it by a record deletion, and it is not out of sequence. Deletion is made by placing a 'delete' marker in the record so that the record can be over-written if desired.

Other techniques for dealing with overflow can be used. For example, in a variable length track format, a record addition is placed in sequence in the home track, the rest of the records moved along one place pushing the last record off the track into an overflow area. One implication in this method is that track indexes have to be modified as the highest key in the track will change. This consideration does not apply in the tag insertion system described above. However, the example given above serves the purpose of illustrating that there must be, in indexed sequential processing, a routine for dealing with overflow situations.

Direct access processing

We have seen that in sequential and indexed-sequential modes of processing direct access can still be obtained to any record through an indexing system. Since direct access processing pre-supposes the storage of data records in random key sequence but still demands access to any individual record on demand, the obvious question to arise is why not store all records sequentially within their file, since, as we saw above, direct access is possible. Two major considerations arise here:

Self-indexing is only a viable proposition where all keys in the file are consecutive, and should there be gaps in the sequence, storage locations must still be allocated.

In an indexed sequential file, tracing a location through a series of indexing levels is a time consuming process.

Now, as far as the first consideration goes, it is seldom we find a key coding system that meets this requirement. A file may be started with a completely consecutive sequence of keys but in the course of time this becomes corrupted by the addition and deletion of records. Gaps and clusters appear resulting in wastage of storage space and involved record overflow tagging. Not only this, but keys constructed as we saw in an earlier chapter, on Significant Digit, Hierarchial of Alpha/ Numeric principle will, by nature, not be a complete sequence of keys. The second consideration gives rise to problems of response time. When record interrogation techniques call for a very fast response time, the lengthy process of searching through level indexes will probably not be acceptable.

One method of getting round these difficulties is to evolve a method where, by the application of some mathematic technique to the record key number, the location address would be automatically generated. Such a technique is known as *address generation* or *indirect addressing*. The measure of the problem may be stated as follows:

The starting point is a range of keys that may not be consecutive and will have gaps and clusters of keys. The format of the keys may differ materially from the format of the location address, for example, more digits, digits may be an Alpha/Numeric mix.

The object is to provide a set of addresses within the range allocated to the file, and to distribute the records evenly over the file locations available. For example, if a bucket principle is used with four records per bucket, to finish the process with every bucket neatly containing four records and so optimise the use of storage space.

Now, in fact, there is no technique that will give a 100 % realisation of these objectives. The best we can do is to design a process that gets as near the objectives as possible. There are, indeed, a number of techniques that can be used, the choice depending on conditions present in any particular application. To review all of these in depth would take a whole book larger than this one, so just one of the simpler methods is given as an illustration.

A file is allocated on 20 cylinders numbered 20-39, each cylinder containing 8 tracks holding 4 buckets each containing 4 records. This gives a total record capacity of 2560 held in 640 addressable buckets. We wish to calculate an address for a record with the key 14936.

If we take the prime number nearest below 640, that is 631, divide it into the key number then the remainder must be within the range 000 to 630. With key reference 14936 the remainder is 423. We can call this number the relative bucket address, which has now to be converted into cylinder, track and bucket address.

If, then, we divide 423 by the number of cylinders, 20, the remainder must fall within the range 00-19, in this case it is 3. By adding 20, the lowest cylinder number, a cylinder address is derived, 23. If now we divide 423 by 32, the number of buckets in a cylinder (8 tracks of 4 buckets) the remainder will be between 0 and 31, giving a cylinder bucket address, in this case, 7. The location address would therefore be expressed as 2307, the seventh bucket on cylinder 23. This could again be taken a stage further by first dividing 423 by 8, with the remainder 7 identifying the track within the cylinder and a further division of 423 by 4 with a remainder of 3 giving the bucket reference in the track. In this case the location address is 2373, bucket 3 in track 7 of cylinder 23.

One problem encountered in any form of indirect addressing is the probability that the same location will be generated for two different key numbers. In the example given above, the key 15567 on being divided by the prime number 631 would have the same remainder 423 and so will address the same bucket. Of course, the problem is reduced if records are organised four to each bucket as this enables four synonyms to be coped with. If, however, we found the same address generated more than 4 times, overflow techniques would have to be used to deal with the situation.

EXERCISES

1. Distinguish between serial file processing and sequential processing, explain why it is impractical to use a self-indexing system with the latter.

2. One aim of organising records on file is to make the most efficient use of variable storage space. Which of three file organisation principles, serial, sequential or direct do you think stands the greatest chance of realising this aim? Give reasons for your decision.

3. What do you understand by an indexed sequential file? Explain how records can be directly accessed using this type of file organisation.

4. A bucket holds four records, keys 4973, 4974, 4985 and 4986, taking up the whole of the bucket storage space. On processing an additional record, 4976 has to be inserted. (a) How would the computer deal with this situation and (b) explain how the machine would deal with up-dating all five records in the next processing run.

5. Self-indexing is only viable when all the record keys are consecutive. Explain why and what would happen if gaps occurred in the key sequence.

12

Hardware Systems

Since the late nineteen forties, when computers first began to be used for commercial data processing, one remarkable factor has been the continual progress in hardware technology and in systems know-how. As new machines are introduced the user, having decided upon a machine and then spent a year or two in system development and planning, on 'going operational' found that the hardware had become out-dated and that new and faster machines had become available. However over the past few years the situation has tended to stabilise and a plateau seems to have been reached in the construction and development in that rather grey area known as medium sized computers. In the commercial world, the main technical diversion from this main stream of computer progress has been the introduction of what are known as small computers; most of which centre around a visible record facility.

The current trend in the pattern of demand would appear to be away from the conventional medium sized machine and moving towards, on the one hand, large configurations offering a service to a number of users simultaneously or dedicated to giving a nation-wide service for one particular application, and on the other hand towards the small office Visible Record machine. With the progression of the more powerful computers have come various terms – *Real-time–Multi-programming–Time-sharing* – to give labels to operating modes, and a number of terms have been associated with small computers at the other end of the scale.

BATCH PROCESSING

Most early computer data processing systems were operated in a batch mode. Essentially this means collecting input records over a period of time, maybe a day, a week or a month, but in any case the records are an account of transactions that have taken place in the past—*historic data.* Records are batched, the batches controlled through control and hash totals, document sequence checks, batch slips etc and are forwarded to the data processing department for processing.

This usually involves an off-line conversion process to a machine readable form (punched cards or punched paper tape) and then writing the records to backing storage. Magnetic tape is commonly used on this processing mode. In turn, these magnetic tape files holding the movement data received in batches, may be built up over a period of time until, for a example, a movement tape is prepared for all transactions during a month and at the end of the month is processed against master files to produce an end product, say, sales ledger accounts.

From a systems point of view, batch processing has one major disadvantage in that the files are never completely up to date. Even immediately after the periodic up-dating, files will still not hold records generated after the last batch processed. On the credit side, batch processing systems are fairly simple in concept, following a clearly defined pattern of data preparation—input, processing, output schedule—and do not demand sophisticated operating techniques.

On the hardware side, machine utilisation is poor. If batch processing is used in serial mode, that is—read-in data from backing store, process, output results to print—then only a very small proportion of the machine's available processing time is being used. This is due to the large proportion of the time spent in the input and output processes.

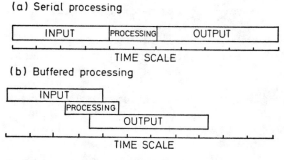

Figure 12.1. *Buffering input and output*

Machine efficiency can be improved by the use of buffering techniques. Non-addressable areas of storage are allocated to receive incoming data and in which to assemble output data. This means that, on a time scale, the input, processing and output functions overlap increasing the proportion of available time spent in processing (Figure 12.1).

MULTI-PROGRAMMING

In the preceding comments on batch processing it was assumed that one program only was available in the computer store for processing purposes. Multi-programming is a situation in which two or more programs are held in store simultaneously and operating control can be switched between them as and when required.

This helps to overcome the disadvantage inherent in either serial or buffered batch processing, i.e. the poor utilisation of processing capacity. With three programs stored simultaneously, one can be using data channels for input, another channel to output data and the third program occupy itself in arithmetic or other processing functions. This means, as shown in Figure 12.2, a far more efficient utilisation of processing time.

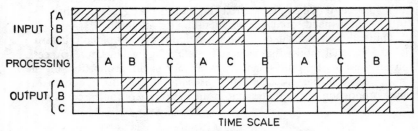

Figure 12.2. Multiprogramming time scale

From a software viewpoint, a highly sophisticated operating system will be required with facilities for:

(a) Allocating control to programs in accordance with a pre-determined priority rating. The program with the highest priority is initially run, but when processing is held up awaiting input of records or disposal of output, control is switched to the program with the next highest priority and not until processing is held up on both is the third program brought in. As soon as the first program is ready to recommence processing, the program being run is interrupted and control switches back to the first.

(b) Housekeeping routines to ensure security of data held in registers when control is switched from one program to another. This is done by temporarily storing in other registers and transferring back when control is returned to the relevant program. Security of the programs themselves to ensure only the correct program can be accessed.

(c) Scrutiny of peripherals to ensure output and input devices are available when required by program, with automatic switching to another program should this not be the case.

Hardware considerations will include:

(a) Provision of a relatively large central processor store to accommodate not only the programs but the operating system.
(b) A wider range of peripherals particularly on-line backing storage to hold files containing records that need to be referenced by all programs in store.
(c) Incorporated in multi-programming processors are special purpose storage registers which indicate the instruction and location currently being processed in each program. This preserves continuity throughout the program in the event of interruption.

An important factor in determining the priority rating of programs is the relationship between central processor time and peripheral time. If the time communicating with peripherals is very high compared with processing time, interrupts will be very frequent and therefore the program is allocated a high priority rating. By the same token, programs using slow input and output devices would have priority over those using fast peripherals.

In some multi-programming systems, programs are allocated a fixed amount of time in rotation, interrupt occurring when the time has expired. However facilities are also incorporated for priority interrupt and should a program be interrupted before its time slice has been used up, control will switch back at the earliest opportunity to make available the unexpired time.

While the cost of a multi-programming configuration is high, it can be justified if the volume and range of work is sufficient to keep the machine working at a high level. It is a type of system that commends itself to computer bureaux dealing with the requirements of a number of users.

TIME SHARING

The essential difference between a time-sharing and a multi-programming system is that, while in the latter, the processor has access to a number of programs, at any one time, in the former a number of users have access to the processor virtually simultaneously. It may, however, be, that a time-sharing system will also work in a multi-programming mode.

Users are provided with remote terminals linked on line to the processor. Terminals are buffered so that input can be held temporarily until the processor is ready to receive it. The operating system conducts a cyclical search around all the terminals allocating processing time in short bursts to users in turn. The user, having input data through his terminal finds the speed of the rotational search and the resultant processing so fast that a virtually immediate output response is received. This gives the illusion that a number of users are using the processor simultaneously.

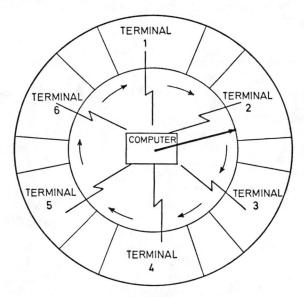

Figure 12.3. Time sharing system

The software requirements of a number of users must be available simultaneously within the central computer configuration. Each user will have their own suite of programs and users may be operating in different computer languages. In the same way, each user will require access to their own systems files. This means that a time-sharing system will have very high volume direct access backing store holding both user programs and files. As a terminal comes on-line to the machine for processing the relevant program must be read from backing store into the processor. After processing it is transferred back to direct access store and the next program demanded called in.

As with a multi-programming system, sophisticated operating systems are required for time-sharing working that will control the search for and transfer of data from terminals and organise access to the wide range of programs and files held in store. The essence of the system lies in the provision of terminals sited on user's premises, connected by transmission lines to the central computer. Different types of terminal will be reviewed later in the chapter.

REAL-TIME SYSTEMS

The most important characteristic of a real-time system is that it is designed to accept data relating to an activity immediately it occurs, to process the data and to output the result quickly enough to have an influence on the activity.

Real-time systems work through terminals that have immediate access to the computer and through it immediate access to the required program and data files. This again means high volume direct access

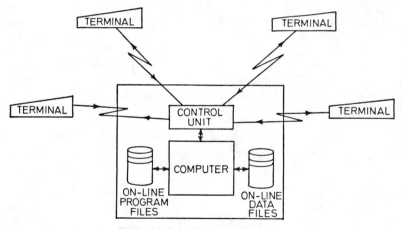

Figure 12.4. Real-time working

storage to hold all the programs and files necessary. As suggested in an earlier chapter, whilst real-time working has an important role to play in many activities where an immediate response is required as a controlling factor, such as in production and process control, it nevertheless plays an important part in some commercial data processing systems (see Figure 12.4).

These applications include file interrogation procedures when, for instance, the balance of a customer's account is required at very short notice, input of movement records where a completely up to date statement of position is demanded by the system such as current stock levels in a stores inventory procedure.

As is the case with a time-sharing system a real-time working mode must be able to accommodate a number of users through on-line terminals virtually processing information simultaneously and immediately.

Multi-access

This is a term used to indicate a system where a number of users have on-line access to the computer through terminals each operating independently. The term is often used both in relation to time-sharing and real-time systems.

Multi-processing

This again is a term that is not very well defined. It usually, however, relates to a configuration in which two or more computers are interconnected by transmission lines. In practice, this often involves a central large machine linked with a number of small satellite computers. These are able to process simple jobs independently in a 'stand alone' capacity but have the power and the storage capacity of the central machine available to call upon.

ON-LINE TERMINALS

There is an extensive range of makes and types of terminal in use. Broadly speaking, they can be classified into the following four main categories:

> Batch processing terminals.
> Teletype terminals.
> Visual display terminals.
> Specialised terminals.

All the above types have in common the fact that they can be connected by transmission line to a central computer although the requirements of the line will depend on the speed of transmission. This subject was dealt with earlier.

Batch processing terminals

These, as the name suggests, are terminals designed to process data in a batch mode. In their simplest form they will consist of a reader,

usually punched card or punched paper tape, a small processing unit
to provide control and buffering facilities and a fairly fast output device
usually a line printer.

This type of terminal is becoming more popular with computer
bureaux. Sited in user's premises it gives the processing power of a
medium sized machine. User files are held centrally on magnetic media,
batched data read to files over transmission lines and the results of
processing fed back to the printer. It is common practice to use this
type of terminal in a time-sharing mode.

Teletype terminals

These are by far the most widely used kind of terminal and consist
of a typewriter keyboard in which data can be entered manually and a
single-character serial printing device. The Teletype is too slow for high
volume data input and its use is restricted to situations where, although
an appreciable amount of processing power is required, input volumes
are small. This type of terminal is suitable for file interrogation procedures and for problem solving where only a few variables need be
input.

Teletype terminals work in what is known as a 'conversational
mode' with messages flowing to and from the computer. For this
purpose special conversational languages have been developed of which
probably the most generally used is BASIC.

An example of the 'Logging-on' procedure for a terminal is as
follows:

1. Using a slightly modified telephone instrument dial the telephone
   number of the computer over the normal GPO network.
2. On contact a high pitched tone is heard—press down the 'data'
   button on the telephone handset—do not replace the receiver.
3. A message from the computer will now be printed on the terminal
   indicating that it is available or otherwise.
4. Type 'LOG' into the keyboard and depress the return key.
5. A further message from the computer asking for a control code.
6. Enter control code and depress return key.
7. The terminal will now ask for a Password. This is the word allocated to the user without which access cannot be gained to programs or files.
8. Password is entered and return key depressed.
9. A message will now come from the computer indicating that the
   machine is ready for use.
10. Enter OLD or NEW depending on whether it is an existing program
    you wish to run or a new program you want to compile.

11. If it is an 'old' program enter the name of the program and depress the return key.
12. If it is a 'new' program enter the name to identify it for future use and press return.
13. In both cases the machine will respond with READY.
14. Variables or data can then be entered manually as requested by the program.

Visual display terminals

Basically these are similar to teletype terminals having keyboard input but instead of a printed output, data is displayed on a cathode ray tube. Data is more easily verified with this device compared with a print out as it is displayed on the screen for rapid visual checking as it is keyed in.

Another advantage is that data can be displayed far more rapidly than in printed form, and can be scrutinised more easily and quickly facilitating the typing back of any message to modify the displayed data. Again this device is not suitable for high volume data transmission and usually finds its role in real-time file interrogating and up-dating procedures.

Specialised terminals

This covers a very wide range of device types, one or two of which have already been mentioned elsewhere. While it is impractical to list the whole range a few examples are given as follows:

1. Monitoring devices used in process control.
2. Document up-dating terminals. For example a building society investment pass-book is placed in a terminal, payments or withdrawals keyed in with customer identification. The account held in a remote machine is automatically up-dated, revised balance transmitted back and printed in pass-book.
3. Magnetic or optical scrutiny devices for reading encoded data on products for immediate up-dating of stock inventory records.
4. Visual display units used, for example, in engineering applications giving diagrammatic representation of projects in various perspectives.

SMALL COMPUTERS

To attempt to define a small computer would be a fruitless task, and to attempt to draw a line between what are known as 'main-frame' computers and the range of machines described as micro-computers, mini-computers, midi-computers and visible record computers is almost impossible. A glance through a selection of machines on the market described as small computers reveals machines with CPU capacities within the 1 K and 124 K range, cycle times ranging from 0.3 to 2 micro-seconds, programming languages from assembler to COBOL and FORTRAN and with interface facilities for a wide range of peripherals.

The purpose of this section is not a detailed survey of micro, mini, midi machines, but rather to review the use in business systems of those small computers with a visible record facility which, incidentally, includes the majority of machines within this range. The use of these machines has expanded dramatically over the past few years and in terms of numbers, now probably represent the largest market for computer systems. There are a number of reasons for this, among which are the following:

1. A VR machine gives the advantage of a limited degree of automation at a comparatively low cost.
2. It retains the conventional 'hard copy' facility, that is a visible record of transactions, easy to read and to understand.
3. It provides storage facilities of varying capacities depending on the configuration, but all machines provide for the automatic input of static data and current record balances.
4. The machine is easy to operate, reducing the need for operator training to a minimum.
5. While batch input facilities are available in many machines, data can be input through a conventional keyboard eliminating the need for elaborate data conversion processes.
6. Systems and program development and construction are rarely needed, these are provided as standard software by the manufacturer.
7. Does not demand the environmental conditions of a large computer, air conditioning, temperature and humidity controls.
8. Fits in with the established order of things. No need for complex data processing department.

The above points apply in a general sense to visible record computers but, as we shall see later, there are levels of sophistication even in these comparatively small machines, providing a wide range of features. Discounting small computers that are used as satellites in a multi-processing situation, two basic levels can be distinguished:

(a) The Visible Record Computer that is basically a development from electro mechanical accounting machines using internal electronic storage to replace the old mechanical program and mechanical arithmetic registers. This gives far greater versatility in programs and greatly varied storage capacity. In many such machines, storage is supplemented by a small backing store in the form of magnetic tape loop cassettes. Input is through a manually operated keyboard for movement data while static and master data is read from magnetic storage in the form of a stripe on the back of the ledger card.

(b) The second is rather like in design, a small main frame computer having a central processing unit with store but also capable of

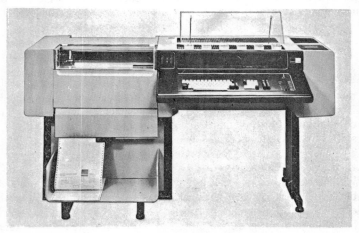

Figure 12.5. A visible record computer (Kienzle Data Systems)

driving a range of peripherals. While keyboard manual input is retained, facilities are available for batch input through card and tape readers. The system will support a line printer for fast output and also backing storage in magnetic disc or tape.

COST BENEFIT

The two ends of the spectrum in data processing systems are manual processing and main frame computer configurations. Generally speaking manual systems continue to be manual because on cost benefit grounds there is no reason for changing although these are usually fairly low volume throughput operations. At the other extreme, cost benefit may not be the only criterion. With very high levels of throughput this may be the only practical way of dealing with the problem within the time limits imposed by the system.

In between the two there is a wide range of commercial applications for which the visible record computer offers an attractive cost benefit ratio. While some reasons for this have already been mentioned earlier in this chapter, important factors tending to make the use of these machines very competitive are:

(a) The visible record computer will usually fit into the normal office situation. It is departmental rather than organisation based. This means:
  1. Little change is needed in the organisation of the department, the machine becomes part of the department rather than the department becoming part of the machine system.
  2. No special environmental conditions are required.
(b) It will probably do the job just as adequately and efficiently as a larger computer in the case of uncomplicated applications. For example, sales ledger, purchase ledger and wages systems.
(c) Operation is relatively easy and to an extent, unskilled. A machine accounting operator should have no difficulty in changing over to a visible record machine and the cost of engaging experienced computer operators is obviated.
(d) While computers, to earn their keep, are often run on a 24 hour shift basis involving large increased expenditure in staffing costs and overheads, VRC's are quite happy to work on a 9-5 basis and it is possibly cheaper in the long run to instal a second machine than to operate for double the hours.
(e) In-house systems and program staff are not required, neither for that matter is a computer manager, control staff or all the rest of the personnel that are normally found to be essential in a computer department.
(f) Naturally with a smaller machine maintenance costs will be less, but on the whole modern VRC's tend to be very reliable leading to quite small time losses during 'down' periods.

ELEMENTS OF A VISIBLE RECORD COMPUTER

It has already been stated that a wide range of small computers with visible record facilities is available today on the market. It would be unreasonable to attempt to describe the 'typical' VRC as no such thing exists. The best that can be done is to review some features that are common to most.

Central processing unit

This performs much the same functions as a larger computer but is on a smaller scale. It holds a control unit to supervise execution of program functions, to control hardware—keyboard, printer and peripherals—and to control flow of data to and from storage to processor.

The CPU incorporates an arithmetic unit that will cope with normal numeric processing, addition, subtraction, multiplication, division and comparison. Immediate access storage capacity varies very much from machine to machine as does also word length, but a capacity of say 8 K of 16 bit words would not be untypical.

Input

This is through manually operated keyboard and magnetic stripe cards in basic models. Interface is provided for faster input devices, punched card and tape.

Figure 12.6. Keyboard — visible record computer (Kienzle Data Systems)

The keyboard is usually in three sections, an alpha/numeric section for input of descriptive data, a ten-digit numeric keyboard for quantitative data and a section containing function keys (see Figure 12.5).

Date	Trans.	Ref. No.	Debit	V.A.T.	Credit	Discount	Balance	Turnover/ Remarks
							50.00	150.00
180276	INV	000002	18.79	1.47			70.26	
80376	CSH	004639			49.25−	3.05−	17.96	168.79

Figure 12.7. VRC ledger card

Many machines incorporate an alpha/numeric line display above the keyboard to give a visual record of data as it is entered. This display line is also used for other purposes such as to show the program stage reached, the condition of the control system or for maintenance test purposes. Static and master data is read from the magnetic stripe on cards as they pass through the machine (Figure 12.7). Data is recorded magnetically on the stripe by keyboard operation and also automatically as output from processing at the end of each card operation cycle.

Output
   Range of output modes will be determined by the peripherals available but common to most machines are:

(a) Output in hard copy form on ledger cards through a printer integrated with the control console. Various types of printer are used. The one common feature is that moving carriages have been dispensed with in favour of a moving type face. One of the faster types of printer uses the constantly moving type face principle of a drum line printer but substitutes for the drum a disc with eight parallel character sets mounted on its circumference. The disc travels backwards and forwards along the length of the printer but, having eight character sets can print eight characters virtually simultaneously.
(b) Output to magnetic stripe storage on ledger cards.
(c) Output to backing storage, magnetic tape cassette or in larger systems to disc or magnetic tape.

Programs
   These are usually held on magnetic tape loop cassette. The cassette is inserted into the machine and the program transferred to store on depression of the relevant function key. Programs can be written to tape or modified by manual keyboard input.
   Program languages used in VRC systems are usually non-standard and are constructed in a fairly basic assembly code. Assemblers are available for their conversion to machine object programs.

Peripherals
   As indicated earlier in this chapter, many VRC systems will support a range of peripherals:
                     Line printer.
                     Punched card reader.
                     Punched paper tape reader.
                     Magnetic disc store.

EXERCISES

1. Using any system with which you are familiar to illustrate your answer, describe what is meant by a batch processing system.

2. Give an account of how a multi-programming system works.

3. What do you understand by a 'Real-time' system? What do you consider to be the main advantages of such an operating mode?

4. Give an account of the different types of terminal commonly in use in data processing systems.

5. Why do you think small Visible Record Computers are becoming increasingly more and more popular?

6. Give a brief description of the main elements of a Visible Record Computer?

7. What do you understand by 'Magnetic Stripe Storage'? Describe an application in which this kind of storage is used.

8. Give an account of how a 'Time-sharing' system works. What additional features are evident in a time-sharing system compared with a Multi-programming system?

9. Give an account of the cost savings you feel would be effected by the use of a Visible Record Computer compared with a larger mainframe machine.

10. What is the importance of operating systems in modern data processing configurations? Indicate the relevance of 'interrupt' and machine/operator communication in this context.

11. What do you consider to be the advantages of a Visible Record Computer for processing accountancy data over a conventional electro-mechanical accounting machine?

13

Applications

The purpose of this chapter is to outline the treatment of some commercial systems applications in which backing storage of a type other than magnetic tape is used. One important business function that is commonly the subject of computer processing is that of sales accounting and stock inventory. The major procedures for this can be identified as follows:

(a) Receipt of customer's order.
(b) Vetting for credit control purposes and opening new accounts where appropriate.
(c) Preparing documents in relation to the execution of the order and despatch of goods, such as stores despatch instructions and customer advice notes.
(d) Calculating the value of goods sold and preparing the invoice.
(e) Up-dating stock inventory file.
(f) Up-dating sales ledger.
(g) Preparing customer sales statements.
(h) Preparation of reports and analyses arising from (e) and (f).

Now it would be quite usual to find that some of the earlier procedures listed would be performed manually with computer processing taking over at a defined point within the system. In the following examples we will assume the point of entry to computer processing to be immediately after the preparation of customer advice notes listing the articles despatched.

SALES LEDGER AND STOCK INVENTORY
The approach to the following systems explanations has been deliberately kept fairly simple in order to avoid obscuring the principles with too much detail. In fact the treatment of only one input document is discussed, the advice note, originating in the despatch department. It has also been assumed that all sales are on a credit basis giving rise to the preparation of an invoice and later to a monthly sales statement of account.

However, it will be appreciated that in a sales ledger system movement documentation will include:

(a) Sales invoices.
(b) Credit notes.
(c) Remittance advices.
(d) Adjustments for bad debts, rectification of errors etc.

and also additions and deductions will be made from time to time to the master file as new customer records are created and as customers drop out. In the same way a number of source documents will be applied to a stock inventory system. These documents include:

(a) Advice notes.
(b) Customer returns notes.
(c) Supplier delivery notes.
(d) Supplier return notes.
(e) Adjustment-stock discrepancies, changed prices etc.

and again, additions and deletions to master file records.

By and large, the treatment of all these movements transactions will be the same as that described for advice notes and invoices. Although addition and deletion of master records would be the subject of separate treatment.

Source documents

Advice notes are prepared by the despatch department, one copy sent to the customer and second copies, containing the following information, batched and sent daily to the computer department.

(a) Customer account number, name and address.
(b) Date and advice note number.
(c) Part numbers and descriptions of goods despatched.
(d) Quantity of each item in (c) above.

Output

Output reports required of the computer system are:

1. Daily   Customer invoices.
                 Re-order list of stock items.

2. Monthly.   Customer sales statements.
                 Sales analysis by areas.

Both sales account numbers and stock codes are significant to a degree. The first two digits of the former indicating the sales area, and the first two of the latter a product group.

Data preparation
'Spread' type punched cards are prepared from advice notes enabling a number of stock items delivered to the same customer to be accommodated on one card. The essential information extracted from the advice note and punched into card is, for the purpose of the illustration, as follows: (a) Customer account number; (b) Stock item code; (c) Quantity.

In practice other information would be included. For example, the advice note number would normally be quoted on the invoice and indeed would be necessary if more than one customer order was being processed in one batch giving rise to the need for more than one invoice. Also, in many cases it would be necessary to quote the customer order number, and perhaps, the date of delivery. Assuming then we restrict the punched information to the three items listed above, the punched record will appear as follows:

Customer
A/c number
12345

Stock item code	Quantity	Stock item code	Quantity	Stock item code	Quantity
2469	24	1369	50	1742	32

Files
Files are held on exchangeable disc packs as follows:

1. *Movement file.* This holds daily movement items read in from punched cards. Initially records will be in random order by customer account number, that is the order in which advice notes are raised by despatch department. Since it will be necessary later on to sort records by stock item number for stock inventory up-dating, to avoid losing the identity of each item with the customer account number, it is necessary to prefix each such item with the customer reference. This is done when records are read to disc with the resulting format:

12345, 2469, 24.   12345, 1369, 50.   12345, 1742, 32.

2. *Master sales ledger file.* This will hold records for every customer on the file containing the following:
    (a) Customer identification—account number, name and address.
    (b) Balance outstanding at the commencement of the months trading with a list of invoice numbers and amounts making up this balance.
    (c) Movement items to date for the current month showing date, invoice number and amount.
    (d) Total balance outstanding to date.

3. *Stock inventory master file.* This will hold a record for each stock item containing the following:
    (a) Stock item identification—stock code and description.
    (b) Control information—minimum and maximum stock levels, stock re-order level and quantity etc.
    (c) Records showing issues and receipts during the current period.

SEQUENTIAL FILE ORGANISATION

Having outlined input and output requirements of the system it is now proposed to examine the computer processing runs (a) with the master files organised sequentially and (b) with an indexed-sequential organisation.

From many points of view, processing in this mode is very similar to magnetic tape file processing. Master records are held on disc in key sequence order in a continuous set of addresses and, before an up-dating run, movement records must be sorted into the same sequence. From a storage point of view, two approaches to up-dating runs need to be considered;

(a) Up-dating records and writing them back to the original disc file area, and
(b) Completely rewriting the file during up-dating to a completely separate disc or file area.

As suggested in Chapter 11, sequential file organisation allows for expanded records that have outgrown their location in store to be placed in overflow store areas with their new addresses tagged and also for additional records to be located in the same way. This makes possible the use of storage in the mode (a) above. However, with a high hit-rate and where records are likely to be substantially expanded in the up-dating process, a situation might well arise when a large proportion of the records have been diverted to overflow areas and home addresses contain a high proportion of tags.

Under these circumstances much of the advantage of fast processing associated with sequential organisation is lost, and it could well be that more rapid processing could be achieved by adopting mode (b) above.

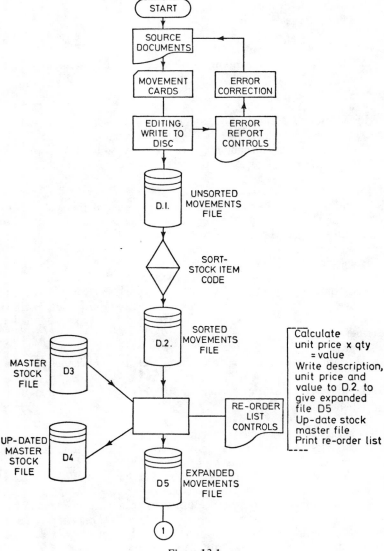

Figure 13.1

That is by completely rewriting all records as processing takes place as is done with magnetic tape storage. It is this principle (b) that is illustrated in Figures 13.1 and 13.2 in which the following computer runs are shown.

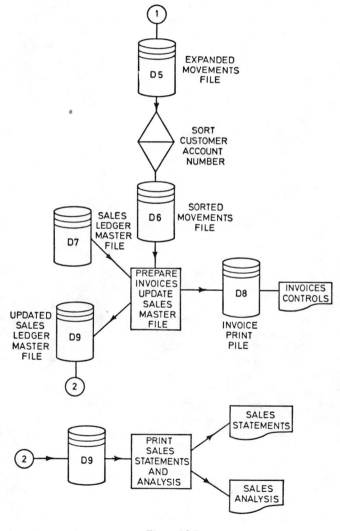

Figure 13.2

1. Data from source documents is punched into cards in the format outlined earlier and records written in random order to disc (D1). Validation and editing procedures are carried out and an error listing printed so that correction can be made and fed back into the system. Editing procedures will include the pre-fixing of each stock movement item with the customer account number to enable reassembly later in customer sequence for invoice preparation.
2. The unsorted movement records are now sorted into stock item code sequence. While this can be done by using the same disc file area and over-writing the unsorted records, a more secure way is to rewrite the records as they are sorted to a separate file area D2.
3. Sorted movements are then processed against the stock inventory master file D3, from which stock item description and unit price are extracted. Calculations are performed to give the product, quantity times unit price, and the record rewritten in its expanded form.

ORIGINAL RECORD

Customer a/c number	Stock item code	Quantity
12345	2469	24

EXPANDED RECORD

Customer a/c number	Stock item code	Description	Quantity	Unit price	Value
12345	2469	2-pint teapots	24	2.50	60.00

In the same run the master stock inventory record is up-dated to give revised stock balances. These new balances are compared with the control criteria governing re-order conditions for each item of stock and a re-order list printed. The up-dated master stock inventory file is completely rewritten to disc file area D4 and the expanded movement records to another area D5.

4. A sort is then made of the records on D5 into customer account number sequence, D6, grouping back together the stock items originally appearing on the advice note.
5. File D6 is then run against sales ledger master file D7 from which the relevant additional information required for the preparation of invoices is extracted. For example, customer name and address and details of discounts and settlement terms. From the interaction of D6 and D7 a print file D8 is prepared from which invoices can later be printed. Master sales records are up-dated being expanded to include invoice identification and total value and revised sales ledger balances calculated.

6. At the end of a month the sales ledger master file will contain records of all transactions relating to the period, from which customer sales statements can be prepared. At the same time totals can be accumulated on the first two digits of the account number for transactions made during the current month and printed to give a monthly sales analysis by area.

The above explanation is an account of sequential processing when, for each run, new files are written. As suggested earlier, an alternative

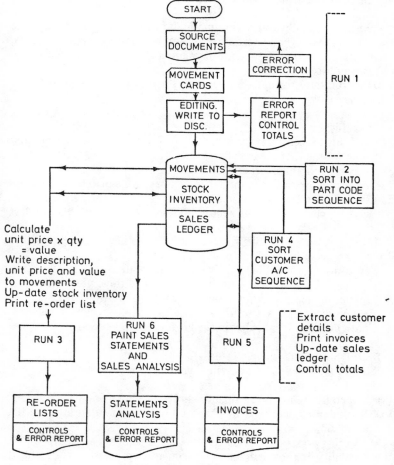

Figure 13.3

way is to over-write the original record with the up-dated record in the same location on the same file area. The main points of difference are:

(a) Updated record is written back to same location on disc or placed if necessary in an overflow area with the home address tagged accordingly.
(b) Records not updated can remain unchanged in their original location on disc.
(c) By and large, the number of runs will be the same but a smaller number of file areas will be required.

Figure 13.3 illustrates this method of processing using disc file areas for sales ledger master records, stock inventory master records, for holding unsorted movement data and a file in which sorted movement records can be held.

The procedure for updating records, shown in chart form in Figure 13.4 is as follows:

1. Open files.
2. Read in to central processor the records contained in the first bucket of the first file cylinder.
3. Read in a movement record.
4. Compare movement and master record keys for a match.
5. If match found update master record.
6. Read in next movement record. If key higher than that of last record in bucket then:
   (a) If creating new file write bucket out to new file area whether any records have been updated or not.
   (b) If using same file area write bucket out to original location only if updating has taken place. If overflow situation results tag and place unaccommodated record in overflow area.
7. Read in second bucket of first cylinder.
8. Continue until final bucket in final cylinder is processed.

INDEXED SEQUENTIAL PROCESSING

Since, in indexed-sequential file organisation records are:

(a) Stored in key number sequence, and
(b) An index as described in Chapter 11 is incorporated into the file structure,

the capability is provided for both sequential processing as described earlier, or for direct access processing by locating any required record

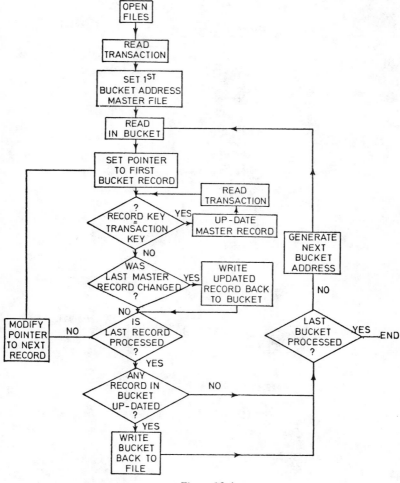

Figure 13.4

by reference to the index. It is, as we have seen, advantageous to use
the former in a high hit-rate situation, but where only a small proportion of the records are to be updated, retrieval of records by direct
access could well represent a more efficient processing mode.

As will be seen from Figure 13.5 illustrating direct access processing
with an indexed-sequential file, one main point of difference is the
elimination of the sorting operations necessary in sequential processing.

180

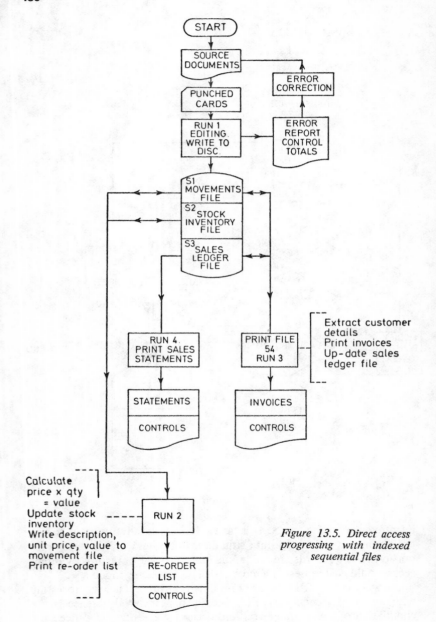

Figure 13.5. Direct access progressing with indexed sequential files

Runs are shown as follows:

1. Cards are read to disc creating a movement file, S1. on which records appear in random order. As before, each record contains customer identification key followed by the stock item codes and quantities of goods supplied. There is no need to prefix each stock movement item with customer account number as was the case with sequential processing as the sequence of records will remain unchanged.
2. The movement file is processed serially. For each movement stock item record, direct access is made to the master record, S2, holding the same key. Processing then follows the same pattern as in sequential 3 above except that the updated master record is written back to its former location on file, over-writing the previous record as indeed is also the expanded movement record.
3. Expanded movement file S1 is now processed in the same way, but this time matching the customer account number with its equivalent directly accessed master record S3. Relevant additional information necessary for invoice preparation is extracted from the master record and a print file S4 written, from which invoices can be printed. Master sales records are updated and written back to their original file location.
4. Customer sales statements and sales analysis are prepared at the end of each month from the sales master file as in sequential 6 above.

The procedure for updating records directly accessed to an indexed-sequential file, shown in chart form in Figure 13.5, is as follows:

1. Open files.
2. Read in to central processor first movement record.
3. Access first track of first file cylinder and read into store the cylinder index.
4. Search cylinder index for key highest above movement record key and form cylinder address.
5. Access first track of this cylinder and read in track index. Search index for key next highest above movement record key and form track address.
6. Access this track and search bucket to locate required record. Read bucket containing record into store.
7. Unpack records, update record sought with movement data.
8. Write bucket containing updated record back to original location on file.

VISIBLE RECORD COMPUTER APPLICATION

It was suggested in Chapter 12 that small visible record computers are becoming more popular and their use fairly widespread for the

processing of commercial systems. A chapter on applications would
hardly be complete without a description of a system on this type of
machine, and the following is an account of the routines involved in
a purchase ledger system.

Purchase ledger system
1. *Hardware.*   This application is based on a fairly basic visible record
   computer. Input is through a manual keyboard and output as hard
   copy on ledger cards through a block printer and also stored in
   coded form in magnetic stripes mounted along the edge of the
   cards (see Figure 12.7). The machine has some backing storage in
   the form of magnetic tape cassettes through which programs can
   be loaded and on which output data can be recorded for future
   processing. While it is appreciated that interface is available on this
   type of machine for a number of peripherals—magnetic disc store,
   line printer, punched card and paper tape readers and punches—it is
   not intended to discuss the use of these, which in any case follows
   much the same pattern as their use with a main frame machine.
   Again, core store capacity will vary in this type of machine from 4 K
   to around 32 K.
2. *Systems objectives.*   Update sales ledger file and produce nominal
   ledger analysis and aged creditors analysis. Prepare remittance
   advice notes and cheques.
3. *Input.*   From source documents—purchase invoices and credit
   notes—through manually operated keyboard, and from stored data
   in magnetic stripe and magnetic tape cassette.
4. *Output.*   Ledger cards printed hard copy with control sheet duplicate.
   Printed remittance advices.
   Printed cheques.
   Nominal ledger analysis.
5. *Files.*   Magnetic stripe containing the following information:
   Ledger card type code.
   Account identification by reference, name and address.
   Balance b/d age analysed over 1, 2 and 3 months.
   Discount total.
   Remittance advice page number.
   Continuation card count.
   Account payment code i.e.

   0 = pay all items
   1 = pay 1 month and over
   2 = pay 2 months and over
   3 = pay 3 months and over

Date (month and year) of last transaction.
15 transaction line entries each containing:

(a) Date
(b) Transaction code (Dr. Cr. etc.)
(c) Nominal ledger code
(d) Supplier's reference
(e) Amount

Count or number of transaction records.

Tape cassette holding:
Programs for reading into store.
Output data for further processing.

Processing
Run 1: invoice and credit note posting.
1. Invoices and credit notes are batched separately and only one type of transaction posted in one run. Documents are pre-listed and a batch slip prepared giving date, batch reference and total value.

2. Variables are entered and held in store—VAT codes and rates, nominal ledger codings and batch date, reference and value.

3. Ledger card with magnetic stripe is fed into the machine. Before the card reaches the 'print' position a validation check is carried out by the operator entering through the keyboard an account identification which is checked against that held in the magnetic stripe.

4. The operator will then key in the following information from the source document:
Account reference number.
Supplier reference number.
Invoice total.
Settlement discount rate.
Date of transaction, and for each invoice item.
Value and nominal ledger code.
VAT code.

After each amount and VAT code has been entered, the appropriate rate will be looked up and the VAT calculated for the item. When all lines have been entered, total value plus total VAT will be compared with the invoice total entered at the start.

5. The following information is now printed on to the face of the
   card:
      Transaction date.
      Type of transaction (e.g. INV or CRN).
      Supplier's reference.
      Amount of debit or credit.
      Updated balance.

   In the case where an invoice is subject to a cash settlement discount,
a second line showing this discount is printed as a debit.

6. In the stripe of the ledger card, the transaction is added to the
   appropriate age analysis month and to the balance carried forward,
   and the following transaction detail stored:
      Supplier's reference.
      Date and month of transaction.
      Amount.
      Transaction type code (e.g. INV or CRN).
      Nominal ledger code (e.g. inventory, capital, expense).
7. Should an overflow situation arise in the magnetic stripe a continuation card will be called for.
8. For nominal ledger analysis purposes details of each transaction
   quoting references, nominal code, value and debit or credit are
   output to tape cassette.
9. It should be noted that, prior to updating the age analysis the last
   posting date will be checked to see if the ageing needs to be moved
   back one or several months.
10. At the end of the run the grand total of the postings will be printed
    out with the original batch total together with any difference between
    the two.
       Nominal code analysis.
       Total of all items printed.
       Total of all discounts taken.
       Total of all amounts to be paid (from remittances).
       Total of all amounts to be paid (from age analysis).

Run 3: Cheque preparation
1. Continuous cheque stationery and blank paper for printing out
   control figures are fed into the machine.
2. Ledger cards for which remittance advices have been prepared are
   inserted in turn and for each one the operator keys in the account
   reference number which is checked against the number stored in
   the stripe.

3. The cheque is now printed by reference to the data stored in the magnetic stripe.
4. The cash posting is printed on the face of the card together with a second line showing the discount claimed.
5. For each cheque the totals produced in the remittance run will be re-calculated and printed on the blank paper as a check against the amount printed in the cheque.

Processing checks
   The following checks are incorporated into every posting run.

(a) *Check digit verification.* A check digit is computed and stored in the magnetic stripe on the ejection of the ledger card. When the card is re-inserted the digit will be computed a second time and compared with the stored digit. Disagreement will signal an error condition.

(b) *Echo check.* Characters recorded on the magnetic stripe will be read a second time and compared with the first reading now in core store.

(c) *Parity check.* On recording a parity bit is set when necessary to make a total number of bits in a frame always odd. On reading, a check for 'odd' parity is made.

EXERCISES
1. A stock inventory file held on magnetic disc contains records organised sequentially. Each record identifies the stock item by stock code number and description, quantity and unit value of stock balance, and details of issues and receipts during the current month. Data items related to receipts quote a job number and quantity issued. Batched requisitions are received from stores daily containing the following information: date, job number, stock item description and stock code number, quantity issued. Only one job number appears on each requisition. Describe (a) How the stock inventory file is updated for stores issued and (b) a routine for printing out an analysis of the value of stock issues per job for each updating run.

2. Give an account of the differences between:

   Processing on a sequentially organised disc file and
   Processing on and indexed-sequentially organised disc file.

Under what circumstances do you think each would be used?

3. Give an account of how data is stored on a ledger card used in a visible record computer. What information would you expect to find on such a ledger card in a sales ledger system?

4. In a sales ledger system what control figures would you expect the computer to print out:
(a) In a run to update the sales ledger from movement records, and
(b) In an invoicing run.

5. Explain the routine for directly accessing a record in a file organised on an indexed-sequential basis.

6. Suggest, giving reasons, the type of backing storage you would use, and the way you would expect records to be organised in store, in the following applications:
(a) Customer sales accounts in an Electricity Board.
(b) A hotel room booking system.
(c) A sales ledger system recording sale of heavy engineering equipment on which there is only movement on 5 % of accounts each month.

14

Management Considerations

The purpose of this chapter is to review a few specific areas in which management has a direct interest and responsibility. The general involvement of management in computer affairs and the problems with which management is faced in changing over from manual to computer processing are dealt with in a separate book on 'Computer Appreciation' by the same author.

ECONOMIC VIABILITY OF COMPUTERS

In arriving at a decision to use a computer within an organisation's administration, a number of factors will have been taken into consideration. One of these doubtless will be an assessment of financial benefits accruing from its introduction but this will not necessarily be the main point of judgement. Among the major benefits expected will be

(a) A better management information service to facilitate planning and control and as a medium to help with policy decision making.

(b) To give a measure of independence from people by automating otherwise manual procedures.

(c) A faster, more efficient and more accurate service to customers.

(d) Reduction of overall data processing costs.

(e) Realisation of indirect savings resulting in quicker turnover of data and report production as well as more effective control of human and machine production resources.

It is difficult to measure objectively the economic benefits derived from a computer, as many subjective factors arise. These can be changed relationships and attitudes on the part of staff and the increase or indeed the loss of goodwill of outside bodies.

However, there are a number of factors which will have an influence on the successful operation of computer services and these are outlined in the following paragraphs.

Applications

A selective approach must be made to applications that could be changed to computer processing, rather than a blanket approach to cover the sum total of all processing requirements. Some procedures may be best processed manually.

For each individual application selection should be made on evidence assembled through a feasability study. Bear in mind that computer personnel are often by nature ambitious and adventurous; the development of a system purely for the interest and sense of achievement it promotes is not in itself a valid reason. Planning control should be at senior executive level not directly involved with computer management.

User satisfaction

It must be remembered that the success of a computer system is measured in terms of the value of the service it provides to the people on the end of the system, i.e. the user, and not in terms of its operational efficiency to the computer department staff. An essential prerequisite to user satisfaction is user involvement. A system designed and imposed upon a user department without reference, through its staff, to departmental requirements is hardly likely to succeed.

While user involvement will necessarily take place during the systems investigation stage, the principle must go further than this. Involvement must promote co-operation on the part of the user, otherwise the system will fail. The user department is essentially part of the system. From here, source documentation will probably be originated, output reports will be used and modifications to the system arising from policy changes will be determined.

In order that users appreciate the purpose and the value of their part, they must be aware of the working of the complete system. It is particularly important to make key user staff aware of the capabilities and limitations of the computer. In the early stages of a project, user education is a most important factor not only in relation to basic computer and systems concepts but also in the advantages expected in their own particular area of work.

Involvement may not necessarily lead to cooperation and indeed cooperation may not necessarily lead to satisfaction; in fact two other ingredients are necessary, goodwill and expertise. The provision of the latter is a managerial function, and the former one that relies on the enthusiasm, persuasion and the general ethos generated on the part of both user and computer department staff.

Performance monitoring

While in the feasability stage, the justification for computer systems will have been established, the performance of the factors on which such justification has been determined must be clearly monitored during development, and implementation. This will mean checking on budgeted costing, the realisation of aims, the accuracy, timeliness and usefulness of outputs. The valuation of performance should be a regular periodic process while the system is operative.

Effective computer management

The success of a computer system will be determined by the quality of the management that controls it. This calls, on the one hand, for technical expertise and experience and, on the other, for the managerial qualities that will promote the welding together of human and machine resources into an effective and efficient working unit.

In the early days of computing, such a combination of attributes was rare, leading often to indifferent performance and a degree of disillusionment on the part of senior management. With the growth in the use of computers over the past few years, such expertise and experience has become more evident and it but remains the responsibility of senior management to ensure that such qualities belong to personnel appointed to computer management positions.

Communication skills

A computer project is essentially a team project where the interchange of ideas and information is essential to the successful development, implementation and continuing performance of procedures. The interaction of the various levels and branches of computer staff, the ability of the analyst to communicate his requirements to the control clerk, the programmer to the operator, all play their part in promoting a successful working relationship.

More important, is the ability of the computer expert to communicate ideas effectively to lay personnel both at user operative level and at higher management level.

Records

The subject of communications cannot be left without reference to the essential need for efficient written records covering all aspects of the system. Without this, the loss of a key member of staff who has kept it all 'in his head' could well lead to chaos.

Systems specification, procedure manuals, operating instructions, in fact the sum total of the objective knowledge on which the whole organisation depends must be effectively documented.

Adverse factors

It would not be wise to leave this summary of factors that have a bearing on the economic viability of computer systems without looking at the converse. A few of the factors that may mitigate against the successful introduction of a computer are given below.

(a) Over-frequent changes in the system or in hardware.
(b) Inadequate testing and implementation procedures.
(c) Over ambition in design of systems. Should it meet every conceivable eventuality or would some exceptions best be dealt with manually?
(d) Insufficient attention given to the design and running of manual support systems, such as collection and transmission of source data.
(e) General reliance on personnel without adequate skills and expertise.
(f) Inadequate ground work in systems investigation.
(g) Over-optimistic conclusions arising from feasibility stage.

AUDIT REQUIREMENTS

With the introduction of computers and computer systems designed to process commercial data, a degree of rethinking had to take place around basic techniques used by auditors in the performance of their duties. Initially a degree of frustration crept into the situation due, on the one hand, to a lack of appreciation of computer processing principles on the part of the auditors, and on the other hand, a failure on the part of computer management and systems design staff to appreciate audit requirements. In recent years, these problems have been largely resolved by the emergence of auditors with a high degree of specialisation in computer processing.

While it is not the province of this book to discuss in detail the respective mandatory responsibilities of management and auditors in this field, a reminder of the demands of company law may help an appreciation of the situation. Essentially an auditor is concerned with an independent review of the company's financial statements and supporting books and records in order to give an opinion as to whether these statements present a true and fair assessment of the company's trading results and financial position. This will enable him to check that the company directors are meeting their responsibilities to shareholders as custodians of the company's resources.

It will be obvious that the auditor cannot meet his responsibilities unless he has access to whatever company records he deems necessary. In the days when all such books and records were kept manually and held as pieces of paper on file or bound in books, tracing and verifying accounts and records was a fairly straightforward business. With records in a computer held on magnetic media, retrievable only through the medium of a computer program, the problem takes on a different significance.

In computer data processing there are three areas in which the auditor will be involved. These are:

Systems approval
Systems controls.
Systems verification.

For the statutory auditor, his checking and verification in a manual system is historical by nature. He is dealing with procedures completed and documents compiled in the past. For the auditor of a computer system it is fundamental that from the inception of the system he should be involved.

Systems approval

The auditor will want to satisfy himself generally, at the systems design stage, of the effectiveness and security of the range of procedures planned. This will include manual clerical procedures outside the computer department to capture and deal with source data as well as procedures determined by program within the computer configuration.

Systems specifications including programs will be adequately documented before the live running of a system, subjected to auditors' test runs and be the subject of formal clearance and acceptance by the auditor. Copies of such specifications and operational programs will be lodged with the auditors as indeed will documented details of any subsequent modification to system or program.

System controls

The auditor will wish to be satisfied that adequate controls exist to safeguard the accuracy of record processing, to safeguard against the possibility of fraud or any other malpractice, and to ensure the security of data within the system. He will also need to be satisfied that precautions are built in to the system to prevent the corruption of data arising from machine malfunction.

A wide range of such controls are available as follows:

(a) *Data preparation controls*
Verification of punched media.
Preparation of control totals for quantitative data.

Use of hash totals to help control transfer of descriptive data.
Document sequence checks.
Document batch control.
Sight validation of source data records.

(b) *Hardware controls*
Read/write checks on data input and output devices.
Read/write checks on record transfer to and from backing storage.
Parity checks on data transfers to and from processor and peripherals and on movements within the processor.
Write permit or inhibit rings for tape files.
Demand for operator intervention in the event of eventually unsuccessful read/write operations.
Operator notification of any malfunction, or irregular situation during processing.

(c) *Software controls*
Validation procedures written into application programs.
Mathematical checks such as check digit verification where appropriate.
Housekeeping packages to control data flow, peripherals to processor, to allocate storage to input and output data, to check file labels and perform block counts.
Executive routines for program lockout to preclude access to wrong program in multi-programming mode.

While the above is not necessarily an exhaustive list of available control techniques is gives an indication of the range of controls at the command of systems designer available to meet the demand of audit requirements.

Systems verification
In a manual system, the process of checking written records through a procedure is relatively straightforward. The whole procedure is usually performed in a progression of quite small steps, providing a trail that can be checked stage by stage by the auditor. Whilst this is a laborious procedure, it does provide evidence of the soundness of the records.

In computer processing however, an audit trail becomes more difficult to follow. From the point information enters the machine to the point at which output reports are prepared there is a gap in which there are no visible readable records. To check data records held on file in the system, the auditor must, therefore, have at his disposal some means of accessing them, and, if required, obtaining hard copies.

We must bear in mind that the chances of processing or arithmetic errors arising in a computer system are extremely remote. If the auditor can satisfy himself in principle that the system is working in conformity with the specifications and programs he has already vetted and agreed, then there is little reason to suppose that there will be fault in individual data records. Methods that might well be adopted to this end are:

(a) Running a standard test pack against a program in every day use and comparing the output with known results.
(b) Selecting at random, programs in every day use and making a comparison run with the copy in the auditor's possession to see if any differences come to light. A special program can be used for this purpose which will only output the differences.
(c) Dumping files on to print so that a visual record is available for checking purposes, although this is a very laborious and wasteful approach.
(d) Examination of copies of computer's console log, identifying programs used on live runs, and also giving details of operator intervention.
(e) Use of special audit program packages to retrieve specific records for examination, to produce reports specified by the auditor, and provide facilities for reporting exceptions. However, such audit packages should be designed to be economical in the use of computer time and also to work within the framework of the configuration being used.

In short, audit routine must be designed to the end that the auditor can be satisfied that all data relevant to the system, and only that data genuinely generated by the system is entered for processing. That all processing procedures called for by the system are being carried through and that such processes are designed in a manner that will ensure accuracy, provide adequate control, and conform with previously specified and agreed procedures.

MANAGEMENT INFORMATION SYSTEMS

A major function of management is to control and a prerequisite of control is information. A management information system seeks to provide such information in a form and at the time that will lead to effective management control.

To discuss in detail the information requirements of all branches and levels of management is too lengthy a process to be described here. The control information needed by the various management functions, production, accountancy, sales, purchasing and so on, as well as the requirements of different levels of management, top, middle and supervisory will vary considerably.

However, we can marshal together a number of basic ideas that are relevant to management information systems and, in particular, think in terms of the benefits which computer processing has brought to this science. Perhaps, reduced to essentials, the major considerations in the provision of information are *timeliness, frequency, degree of detail,* and *distribution;* although it is difficult to divorce these considerations completely from each other.

One major advantage apparent in the use of computers is the speeding up of the processing cycle, not only by reducing the number of procedural stages involved, but by performing basic clerical functions far more quickly. In many manual systems the production of control information is such a lengthy business that, by the time the information is available, the opportunity for effective control is passed. Often the information has to be assembled and consolidated through a series of operational levels before the total picture can be presented to management. With a computer, providing all the records needed are held on file, this is a one-stage process. On the question of timeliness many arguments have centred around the value of real-time management information systems as a material aid to control. Doubtless such arguments will continue for some time yet.

The thought of management having information immediately available through a visual display unit mounted on their desks has its appeal. In fact looked at realistically there are some applications in which a very fast response to enquiries can be of great value. For instance, in a bank, to have at a moment's notice a statement of a customer's balance, for a sales manager to obtain within a very short time an analysis of sales by areas, for a credit control manager to obtain quickly a customer's credit history, could indeed, in some circumstances be critical control techniques.

The currency of output information from a system however can only be as good as that of its input, and real-time systems of this nature are very expensive and complex. Weighing these factors against alternative means of producing management information such as daily lists of account balances, daily sales analysis, daily lists of overdue accounts, circulated to the relevant managerial staff, the viability of a real-time approach in a general sense becomes questionable. Sufficient perhaps to say that computer systems make available techniques for providing, in one way or another, control information to management in time for it to be acted upon.

To lay down hard and fast rules governing the frequency with which reports should be produced would, of course, only be valid in respect of specific situations. In some cases, as for example, the two quoted above, bank account balances and overdue accounts, a daily listing could well be necessary, while an analysis of sales by area could well be required at no greater frequency than one month. Reporting frequency is an important consideration, but can only be determined within the framework of the particular activity it is sought to control.

The question of the degree of detail incorporated into management reports and indeed their format, raises one or two interesting considerations. By the nature of things, the sheer volume of listings and summaries a computer is able to churn out in print can be overwhelming. Should management information only be the systems product of routine computer runs in a summarised form, or should management information be a system in its own right? Again, this is a question that can only be answered in the light of managerial requirements coupled with the hardware and software available. Information is derived from files and a comprehensive management information system in its own right pre-supposes the on-line availability of all relevant files.

The degree of detail required for management purposes is again an instance where the answer must be qualified. The principle of management by exception is well established and indeed for management to concern itself primarily with those areas in which performance has diverged from expectations. But where does exception reporting start and finish with varying levels of management? Generally speaking the lower the level of management, the greater the degree of detail required. To institute action, a budget report at top management level may just highlight that, of the organisations departments, sales performance has fallen outside its budgeted variance.

For the sales manager, more detailed information would be called for, perhaps a breakdown of sales over branches, highlighting again those branches failing to meet their target. The branch manager will probably require in his turn sales statistics down to individual salesman level. It is in this type of reporting that the computer comes into its own with its capacity not only to analyse and produce reports quickly at the various levels of detail demanded, but also to discern within pre-determined parameters those items of information to which notice should be directed.

Whatever degree of detail may be required at varying management levels, a common factor is that information must be clearly presented. While it could well be that the most striking form of expression is in visual display form, we have already seen that this has its limitations.

The great bulk of management information is in printed form prepared on a line printer. Computer printouts can be monotonous in appearance and time-consuming to interpret. A little forethought on editing procedures should lead to the production of reports conveying information clearly, concisely, and making an impact on the user.

Finally, some thought and planning must be given to the distribution of reports. Security, need and cost are three important factors to be taken into account although prestige plays its part. Much of the management information produced is confidential whether it relates to performance from a global, departmental and even individual aspect, and the circulation restricted to nominated staff. The computer department will keep distribution lists for all of the reports it produces.

Apart from the question of confidentiality, is there any point in circulating reports to management on activities outside their own particular area of responsibility? Again, it is impractical to formulate a hard and fast rule. Communications are a vital part of the management process and an important tool in the construction of an effective management team. To stimulate co-operation and ideas it may be a good thing, where practical, for management at executive level to have an overall picture of the organisation's activities and problems. Lower levels of supervisory management, however, will be almost exclusively concerned with receiving just that information which enables them to exercise effective control and planning over their own local areas of responsibility.

The above comments have rather concentrated on management information emanating from, in one form or another, data records of activities that have already taken place. However, this brief survey of management information systems would not be complete without mentioning the use of a computer in providing information on activities while they are happening, and indeed information used to forecast what may happen in the future under specified conditions.

An example of the former is *process control*. This is a technique that uses measuring or monitoring devices to feed to the computer statistical data relating to a manufacturing process while it is taking place. A mathematical representation of the essential variables within which the product must fall is stored in the computer. The computer is programmed to feed back to the machine, or communicate to the machine operator corrective instructions, should the monitoring devices show that the process has fallen outside pre-determined tolerances. Examples of process control are the control of paper thickness as it comes off a mill or control of the mix of ingredients in paint making. The type of computer used in process control is usually analogue, or a hybrid machine using digitally controlled analogue devices.

In the second case, that of projecting probable results of future courses of action is known as *simulation*. Basically, it means constructing mathematical models to represent a real situation applying to these various parameters to indicate varying conditions and getting the computer to work out the probable results arising from these situations. Simulation is a useful tool in attempting to forecast future business trends arising from changes in design and activities and thus provides a useful element in management information systems as a guide to long term decision making.

Another important aid to management in which computer will play its part is in Network Scheduling Techniques, PERT (Program Evaluation and Review Technique) and CPA (Critical Path Analysis). In a complex project involving bringing together a range of resources to co-ordinate with a program of activities at critical times, these techniques seek to specify the optimum resource activity path, or program, resulting in the most effective performance and completion of the project. Standard computer programs are available for use in these techniques.

MANAGING SECURITY

Three areas of management responsibility of general security interest are outlined below.

Security of records

The destruction or corruption of computer records held in magnetic storage media is a real possibility. The volume of records held in a very small space, tape or disc, means that even a minor incident could have very far reaching effects and the reconstruction of such records would be a most expensive and time consuming business, even presupposing that such a reconstruction was even possible.

The obvious precaution is to keep duplicates of data files and programs, or to ensure that the facilities for reconstruction are always available. To store such duplicate records remote from the computer installation precludes the destruction of both copies in the event of a major incident. In the case of magnetic tape files, the grandfather, father, son principle will provide back-up records to rewrite current tapes. For disc files the periodic dumping of records to magnetic tape will again provide the means of reconstructing the files.

Security of information

The interests of the organisation can be severely damaged by unauthorised access and interrogation of records. Details of customers, costs, operating data, future plans, can be of value to a competitor.

With the increased use of remote terminals over the past few years, the possibility of unauthorised access has increased.

Security of assets

It has been said that if a person knows enough about a system he can always beat it. This comment has been proved true many times in the past of computer systems whereby manipulation of a program by by-passing procedures within the system, or by the inclusion of un-authorised data, major frauds have been perpetrated.

Formulation of standards

In general terms, the answer to security problems of the nature outlined above, lies in the setting and the maintenance of standards. To devise the first may be complex and expensive, to enforce the second, difficult. Nevertheless, to protect the interests of the organisation and the individuals within it the formulation of standards is desirable, and should cover the following areas:

1. To minimise the possibility of errors in all data processing systems.
2. To protect the interests of the company in its relationships with customers and suppliers. For example, to safeguard against the non-payment of debts or fraud.
3. To protect against malpractices by computer or user staff.
4. To prevent the unauthorised use of information accessible by computer staff.
5. To ensure that statutory requirements are complied with—company law, statutes relating to employment, statutory wage deductions etc.
6. To meet audit requirements.
7. To provide effective management control information.
8. To specify detailed procedural standards for all processing operations.
9. To provide a framework of rules within which computer staff must work in order to control access to hardware and software and prevent any unilateral action that could result in a malpractice.
10. To define duties and responsibilities within the Computer Department.

EXERCISES

1. Describe the controls you feel should be imposed during the data preparation stage of a system to ensure that data is accurate and complete.
2. Outline the purposes of a management information system.
3. What measures do you feel are available to an auditor to verify that a system is running in the way it was designed to operate?

Index

Access-time, discs, 80, 83
Acoustic coupler, 21, 46, 47
  output, 52
Address generation, 151, 152
  levels, discs, 138
  modification, 118
  symbolic, 107
Addressing, indirect, 151
  magnetic disc, 137
Algol-60, 4
Analogue computers, 10, 11
Application packages, 111
Applications, direct access, 180
  indexed sequential, 178–180
  sequential, 173–178
  VRC, 181–185
Assembly language, 107
Audit, 190–193
  system controls, 191–192
  systems approval, 191
  systems verification, 192–193
Autocode statements, 108
Automatic data transmission, 20

Backing storage, 72–92
Bar coding, 37
Basic, 110, 111, 161
Batch processing, 15, 154, 155, 160
Baud, 20, 47
Binary number system, 22, 24
  BCD, 24
  coded octal, 27
  complement, 24
  conversion, 23, 24
  floating point, 29
  fractions, 24
  pure, 22
Binary numbers in CPU, 60
Block code, 100
Blocking records, 141
Branch instructions, 68–69
Bucket, disc, 84
  home, 85, 86, 148
  overflow, 85, 86, 148

Buffering input and output, 155
Buffer store, 40–41

Calculators, desk, 9
Cash till, 36, 37
Central processor, 12, 56–58
  programe storage, 63
  storage, 58, 61–63, 103
Chain printer, 45
Check digit verification, 184
Cobol, 108, 109
Codes, data records, 99
Communication lines, 19, 20
  satellite, 20
  skills, 188
Compiler, 108–110
Computer/operator communications,
  114
Computers, analogue, 10
  basic configuration, 12
  basic functions, 59
  digital, 11
  economics, 187–190
  files, 97, 98, 134
  hybrid, 11
  instruction code, 106
  limitations, 57, 58
  management, 188
  small, 162
  storage words, 25, 26
  visible record, 162–168
  working efficiency, 13, 14, 70, 155
Computer Bureaux, 17
Controls, 191, 192
Co-ordinate indexing, 103
Cylinder, disc storage, 87, 138–139
Cylinder level index, 146

Data, capture, 18, 19, 129
  control, 94
  conversion, 18
  dynamic, 94
  preparation controls, 190

199